Characters with Character

Using Children's Literature in Character Education

Diane Findlay

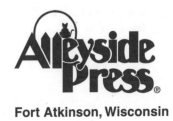

Alleyside Press®

Fort Atkinson, Wisconsin

Acknowledgments

I have many wonderful friends. Most walk on two legs. But some live between the two covers of a book. I've always been an avid reader, and some of my best moments have been spent sharing books with my children, and now, my grandchildren. Being able to combine that love of books with ideas for teaching children skills that will make their lives happier and more productive is a real joy for me.

I couldn't have managed the job without the help of several public libraries, which I consider to be among our country's most underappreciated resources! I appreciate the excellent collection and helpful staff in the West Des Moines Public Library Children's Department, and I salute the staff of one of the best little libraries around, the Waukee Public Library, who took a real interest in this project and provided service above and beyond the call of duty.

Published by **Alleyside Press**, an imprint of Highsmith Press
Highsmith Press
W5527 Highway 106
P.O. Box 800
Fort Atkinson, Wisconsin 53538-0800
1-800-558-2110

© Diane Findlay, 2001
Cover design: Debra Neu Sletten

The paper used in this publication meets the minimum requirements of American National Standard for Information Science — Permanence of Paper for Printed Library Material. ANSI/NISO Z39.48-1992.

Library of Congress Cataloging-in-Publication Data
Findlay, Diane, 1952-
  Characters with character : using children's literature in character
education / Diane Findlay.
     p. cm.
Includes bibliographical references and index.
  ISBN 1-57950-064-1 (alk. paper)
 1. Moral education–United States. 2. Character–Study and teaching
(Elementary)–United States. 3. Children's literature,
American–Bibliography. I. Title.
  LC311 .F45 2001
  372'.01'14–dc21
                              2001003463

Contents

Introduction

Character education, and its role in our schools, is attracting increasing attention and support in the dialog between educators, parents and other community leaders. While the range of ideas about character education is wide, a simple expression of the underlying principle is offered by the Center for the 4th and 5th Rs in New York:

> *"…there are universally important ethical values such as respect, responsibility, trustworthiness, fairness, caring, courage, self-control, and diligence. Character means living by these core values—understanding them, caring about them, and acting upon them."*

Character education, at its most universal, involves consciously nurturing in students core ethical values, which can be seen as basic skills for productive, successful living in a diverse and rapidly changing world.

There are many ideas about which values to stress, and about how to teach them in the classroom. However, few would disagree that our homes and schools are places rich in human interactions; and that we want those interactions to be characterized by qualities such as honesty, fairness, respect and responsibility. It can also be said that these positive character values make for happier individual students and teachers, and a more harmonious, orderly and productive learning experience. The reverse also seems to hold true. A lack of these qualities in homes and classrooms produces opposite results. In fact, if we accept the premise that example is a powerful teacher, we can hardly escape the idea that parents, students and teachers teach character values every day—for better or worse—by the example of their own actions.

As the teaching of character values becomes more conscious and systematic, tools that help teachers, librarians and parents present the concepts and nurture the skills and behaviors of good character can contribute to that process. *Characters with Character* is just that sort of tool. It helps students focus on ten basic qualities of good character, with a chapter devoted to each quality. It gives examples of how these qualities look and feel in action, and offers stories, ideas, games and activities for understanding and practicing them.

In *Characters with Character*, good books are used as the springboard for exploring character values in an enriching and lighthearted way. The books listed are the best examples the author could find in the riches of contemporary and classic children's literature, and include reading levels by grade. I encourage you to add your own favorites to the list, and to adapt the activity ideas to suit yourself, your students and your situation. Both the books and the activities are intended to suggest links to subjects across the curriculum, and to be used in a variety of groupings and settings. Each chapter includes discussion prompts, games, creative expressions and miscellaneous activities from the simple to the complex.

The books listed are award-winners, highly recommended, long-loved or simply favorites of the author. All are in print or readily available in libraries. The high-quality titles offer a balance of grade and reading levels, cultures and traditions and level of overt or subtle consequences of characters' choices. The books range from silly to serious and from everyday lives and biographies to fantasy. They were selected for their ability to help deepen and broaden students' understanding of important character traits.

Because exploring and practicing character values involves reflecting on and sharing individual attitudes and experiences, some of the activities in this book ask students to reveal their personal thoughts and feelings. Some students will find this more comfortable than others. Different personalities, experiences and levels of self-expression skills will all come into play as individuals decide how to participate. It is important that you do all you can to keep the learning environment emotionally safe and non-threatening. In some of the activities, specific tips are offered to help accomplish this. But it is up to your sensitivity and knowledge of the students to choose and adapt activities to suit the emotional needs of your group. By doing so, you model responsibility, respect and caring.

1 Responsibility

People who are *responsible* accept the results of their actions. They think ahead, figure out how an action might affect themselves and other people, and choose to do what will be best for themselves and for others. They don't make excuses or blame others for their behavior. They do what they say they'll do, and they accept the rewards or punishments that follow because of their choices. A "responsibility" can mean an important job given to someone who can be counted on to be responsible.

You act *responsibly* when you:

- choose not to sneak extra cookies, because you know you might get a stomachache.

- don't whine about being sent to bed early because you didn't clean your room.

- wait your turn on the slide, so you won't hurt the person going down before you.

- work hard to clean up your classroom now, so you'll be able to go out for recess and play with your friends later.

- keep your promise to do your homework right after school, even when your parents aren't there to remind you.

- take time to feed and walk the dog before you leave for soccer practice.

- *Angel in Charge* by Judy Delton. Houghton Mifflin, 1999. 3–5. Ten-year-old Angel finds herself in charge of the house and her four-year-old brother when Mom leaves on vacation and the sitter breaks her leg.

- *The Big Deal* by Alison Cragin Herzig. Viking, 1992. 2–4. When fourth grader Sam is in danger of losing the pet dog that's too big for him to control, he has to use his brain. An entertaining series of mishaps leads to a solution that helps both Sam and his friends.

- *Cecil's Story* by George Ella Lyon. Orchard Books, 1991. K–5. This dream-like "what if" story expresses the fears and feelings of a young boy. His mother has gone to tend his father, a wounded Civil War soldier, and left him in the care of neighbors.

- *Duck Boy* by Christobel Mattingley. Atheneum, 1986. 3–5. Adam, on vacation with his older siblings on a farm in Australia, feels left out when his brother and sister find exciting things to do. Then he discovers a pair of ducks, with a history of bad luck raising a family. Adam is determined to see that the eggs hatch this time, and goes to work to achieve his goal.

- *Fourth of July* by Barbara Joosse. Alfred A. Knopf, 1985. K–2. Five-year-old Ross is tired of being told he's too young to do the things he wants to do. Marching in an Independence Day parade gives Ross the chance to prove that he can act like a six-year-old.

- *Jamie's Turn* by Jamie DeWitt. Raintree, 1984. K–5. This autobiographical story was written when Jamie was twelve, and chosen as the Raintree "Publish a Book" contest winner. Jamie tells of having to act quickly to save his stepfather Butch's life in a farming accident, and of taking over the chores through Butch's long recovery.

- *Maizie* by Linda Oatman High. Holiday House, 1995. 4–5. Maizie has a lot to deal with for an eleven-year-old—Mom took off, Dad is distant and unreliable, there's never enough money, and she has to take care of her younger sister. But her hope, determination and strength help Maizie let go of the past and make some dreams come true.

- *Marvin Redpost: Alone in His Teacher's House* by Louis Sachar. Random House, 1994. 2–4. Marvin struggles, as the responsibility of tending his teacher's dog in her absence poses big problems.

- *Not so Fast, Songololo* by Niki Daly. Puffin Books, 1994. K–2. Songololo goes with his old granny Gogo to help her shop in the city. He helps her board the bus, cross the street, and carry her things. Gogo surprises him with a new pair of shoes he admires, to replace his worn hand-me-downs.

- *Pedrito's Day* by Luis Garay. Orchard Books, 1997. K–3. Pedrito shines shoes in the market to help his family get by, but his dream is to save enough for a bicycle. When he gets distracted from an important errand and loses Tia Paula's money, he decides he must tell her the truth and replace what he lost from his bicycle savings.

- *Rachel Carson* by Eve Stwertka. Franklin Watts, 1991. 3–5. Highlights from the life of this pioneering woman scientist and writer, who stunned the world with her 1962 book *Silent Spring*, are shared in this biography. The author tells of Carson's dedication to warning us of the dangers of treating our physical environment irresponsibly.

- *Ramona Forever* by Beverly Cleary. Camelot, 1995. 3–5. Everyone loves Ramona! In this book, Ramona and her family grapple with career changes, job worries, latchkey kids, the death of a pet, a family wedding, and the birth of a baby—all in characteristic Quimby style.

- *Saint George and the Dragon* retold by Margaret Hodges. Little, Brown and Company, 1984. K–5. Sir George answers the princess' call to slay a dragon that is terrorizing her people. His courage and faithfulness to his promise earn him the princess' hand in marriage, and sainthood. Adapted from Edmund Spencer's *The Faerie Queene*.

- *Sammy Sosa* by Gabriel Flynn. The Child's World, 2000. 1–3. The 1998 National League's Most Valuable Player, from the Dominican Republic, is featured in this series biography. Along with his spectacular baseball accomplishments, the book emphasizes Sosa's hardworking childhood, and his generous and responsible sharing of his wealth with his poor countrymen.

- *The Signmaker's Assistant* by Ted Arnold. Dial Books for Young Readers, 1992. 1–2. The signmaker's young helper goes a bit crazy with power when he discovers people DO what signs say. He must own up to his actions and make things right with the signmaker and his neighbors.

- *The Story of Lightning and Thunder* by Ashley Bryan. Atheneum, 1993. K–3. Thunder and Lightning are living as sheep near an African village. Son Ram Lightning's thoughtless behavior begins to hurt the village. In consequence, he and Ma Sheep Thunder are sent away to live in the sky, where they will do less harm.

- *Summer Wheels* by Eve Bunting. Harcourt Brace, 1996. 3–5. Young boys in a poor neighborhood experience the consequences of responsible and irresponsible actions, as they deal with a kind man who repairs damaged bicycles and loans them to children.

- *Tink in a Tangle* by Dorothy Haas. Albert Whitman & Company, 1984. 2–5. Tink keeps getting into trouble. She reasons that it's all because of her red hair. After a hilarious set of mishaps, Tink's Mom and her school principal help her redirect her ill-considered schemes.

- *Wagon Wheels* by Barbara Brenner. HarperTrophy, 1993. 1–3. Three young brothers go with their parents to settle on the Kansas frontier, losing their mother on the way. They work hard and struggle, and are kept from starvation by Osage Indians. Their greatest challenge comes when their father goes on ahead to find a better home, leaving them to stay by themselves and then travel alone to join him.

Other Media

- *Horton Hatches the Egg* by Dr. Seuss. Sony, 1984 (videocassette). K–5. Horton the elephant doesn't know what he's getting into when he agrees to tend the egg in lazy Mayzie's nest so she can take a break. But he keeps his word, in spite of enormous obstacles and with surprising results.

- *Put on Your Green Shoes* from the Sony Kid's Music series. Sony, 1993 (CD). K–5. Upbeat songs by popular artists that encourage environmental responsibility.

- *Strega Nona* by Tomie dePaola, from The Tomie dePaola Video Library. 9 minutes. Weston Woods, 1997 (videocassette). K–3. In this award-winning contemporary classic, Big Anthony has to suffer the consequences of his poor choice when he disobeys Strega Nona's warning to never touch her magic pasta pot.

Responsibility Activities

Discussion Prompts

Use the following prompts to guide discussions about responsibility.

▲ **Lean on Me.** Ask, "Who do we count on, at home and at school, to do important things for us like protecting us and keeping us safe, helping us when we're sick, helping us learn, keeping our surroundings clean, feeding us, etc.?"

▲ **Size It Up.** Responsibilities can seem very small, about the right size or too big! Talk about the responsibilities faced by characters in the books listed. Do they seem too small, too big, or just right? Ask students for their ideas about what size responsibilities seem fair for children their age.

▲ **Responsible Pet Ownership.** Several of the books on the list involve caring for animals (i.e. *The Big Deal, Marvin Redpost, Duck Boy*). Ask students how many have pets or animals at home, and if they help care for them. Talk about how caring for an animal can teach and demonstrate responsibility.

▲ **"If I Had a Million Dollars…."** Sammy Sosa chose to use part of the money he earned in professional baseball to help people in his home country, the Dominican Republic. Have the class identify, from the book specific ways Sosa has used his wealth to help people. With Sosa's example in mind, have students suggest ways they might share some of their wealth if they had a million dollars. Point out that you don't have to give away all of your wealth to be responsible.

▲ **Responsibility in Advertising.** Share examples of advertisements from television or magazines. Ask students for their ideas on whether the advertisements encourage people to act responsibly or irresponsibly.

Creative Expressions

Have fun with these creative ways to process concepts from the books on the list.

▲ **An Ode to My Responsibilities.** Have students share the things they are responsible for at home, then work together as a class or in small groups to create a poem, song or poster about their collective responsibilities.

▲ **"I Know Someone Who…."** Have students tell or write, and illustrate their own stories about someone they know being responsible, and share them with the class.

▲ **"I Saw the Sign"** Review with students the signs created by Norman in *The Signmaker's Assistant* that got him in trouble. Have each student think up and create a sign for the classroom that will help everyone behave responsibly.

▲ **Diorama.** Divide the class into groups of four. Each group will create a diorama of a scene from a selected book. Assign one person from each group to create the character figures, one to cut out the figures, one to decorate the background "set" for the diorama, and the last to put the whole thing together. Groups may share ideas and talk to each other throughout the process, but each student must fulfill his own responsibility alone. Each group will share their diorama with the rest of the class. In addition, each group of younger elementary students should talk with the teacher about how the members worked to carry out their responsibilities. For older elementary classes, all students should write brief evaluations of how well they and their teammates fulfilled their responsibilities.

▲ **Group Skits.** Read or review *The Story of Lightning and Thunder*. Have half the class create paper masks to wear to portray Ma Sheep Thunder, and the other half masks to be Son Ram Lightning. Assign Lightning and Thunder teams, and have each team develop a skit in which Son Ram Lightning wants something, and crashes his way through ("biff, bam, butt") to get it. Then Ma Sheep Thunder will follow him with advice on a "better way to use his head." You may want to use bigger groups to develop skits, and help them as needed. Additional students in the groups might play other characters in their particular skit.

▲ **Responsibility Journal.** Have students decorate the front of a journal notebook. At the end of each day during this unit, give them a few minutes to write in their journals. They might start each day's entry as follows: "Today I was responsible in these ways…" This journal could be continued for each character element in the book.

Science Experiments

The book, *Rachel Carson,* warned us of the dangers of treating our environment irresponsibly. An important environmental problem we still face in the world today is water pollution. Use these experiments to demonstrate the harmful effects of water pollution on plants and animals.

▲ **Chemical Pollutants.** When waste and harmful chemicals are dumped onto the ground or into the rivers, they can make their way into all the living things that need water to survive. Follow these steps to demonstrate how pollutants get from the water into the plants that other animals and we use for food.

1) Gather two clear glass jars, a small container of food coloring (blue shows up well), a small sharp knife, some white flowers and a stalk of celery.

2) Pour a small amount of food coloring and an equal amount of water into each glass jar.

3) Cut the ends of the stems off the white flowers, and stand them up in one jar. Cut the stem end off the stalk of celery, and stand it up in the other jar.

4) Leave them for several hours.

5) Notice how the plant absorbs the food coloring as it drinks the water it needs and is discolored. If the pollutant is a harmful pesticide, fertilizer or waste product, it may make the plant sick or even kill it.

▲ **Detergent Pollutants.** Swimming birds, like ducks, float on the water because of the natural oil on their feathers, which makes them waterproof and prevents their feathers from getting soaked and weighing them down. Demonstrate what happens when soap products make their way into the water where these birds live.

Note: You may want to practice this demonstration a time or two. Especially if you're using feathers from land birds, that you have to treat with oil, it can take some experience to get the right amount of oil on the feathers and detergent in the water.

1) Gather a large bowl, a tablespoon of cooking oil, two tablespoons of liquid dish detergent, a spoon, 4–6 feathers (preferably from water birds) and a twist tie or small rubber band.

2) Fill the bowl with water. Add the cooking oil. Show students how the oil spreads out over the surface of the water.

3) Add one tablespoon of the detergent, and stir gently with the spoon to mix, but not to make bubbles. Observe how the detergent breaks up the oil.

4) Empty the water and clean out the bowl. Refill with more water.

5) Now make your "duck" by fastening the feathers together with the twist tie or rubber band, as shown below.

Note: If you're using feathers from a land bird, you will need to coat them lightly with a kitchen vegetable oil spray to get the waterproof effect.

6) Place your "duck" in the water. The oil on the feathers makes them water repellent, so they will float on top of the water.

7) Add the rest of the detergent to the water, and watch what happens.

8) Explain that the "duck" sank below the surface of the water because the detergent broke up the oil on the feathers. A real duck will sink if detergent breaks up the natural oil on its feathers. Without the oily surface, the duck's feathers get soaked through, and the extra water weight drags the duck under.

Talk with students about how they can help prevent harmful pollutants from getting into our water. They might encourage their families to use earth-friendly cleaning products, and to use only natural, non-toxic chemicals in their gardens. They can make sure that they take home their picnic messes, rather than using cleaning products in lakes or rivers. Encourage students to come up with more ideas for helping to keep our water clean.

Games

Use these games when students need a change of pace or a lighthearted break from the work of the day.

▲ **"Red Hair and Other Excuses."** Tink (*Tink in a Tangle*) blames her troubles on her red hair. What excuses do *you* think of when you get in trouble because of something you've done? Offer some examples (i.e. "The dog ate my homework," or "A Martian came to learn about earth and messed up my room looking at my things"). Have students come up with funny, creative excuses. Write them on the board. Then have students vote for the most creative excuse. Be sure to follow up the fun with a brief discussion to clarify that creative excuses may be fun, but won't "work," and don't change the fact that we're all responsible for our behavior.

▲ **"Cause and Effect."** This game gets children moving around, while helping them make the connection between cause and effect. It can move fast to bring a distracted class to attention, and be used spontaneously on and off throughout the day. The first time, you'll need to explain the game and go through several examples. After that, you should be able to signal a round by simply saying, "Quick now, Cause and Effect," and giving an action or choice as a "cause." Start with some action with a likely consequence. Give hypothetical examples, so no one is singled out and publicly ridiculed. For example: "Tim (not a name in this class) didn't get his morning assignment done during study time." Then ask for a possible consequence. Students raise hands. The first one with a hand up gets to provide a consequence—perhaps, "So he has to stay in at recess to finish." If it is reasonable, the teacher says, "Go," and the student gets to retrieve a reward from a basket. Rewards could be candy, stickers, or slips of paper listing privileges. If the student's response is not a reasonable "effect," the teacher says "Another," and goes on to another student, until a reasonable answer comes out. The teacher quickly presents another "cause." Have fun with this. Sprinkle in some silly or fantastic causes. "A clown landed a hot air balloon in the room during the spelling test," might stimulate some creative responses. Three or four quick rounds at a time should wake up the room and provide good food for thought.

▲ **"Where Do You Stand?"** This game also gives students a chance to move, while thinking about responsible choices. Start with four different-colored sheets of poster board, and mark one sheet "1," the next "2," then "3" and the last "4." Line them up on the classroom floor. Then present a series of scenarios, with 4 possible responses. For example, you might say, "Jennifer wants a shirt she saw at the mall, but they cost more money than she has. Should she: 1) Take them when she

thinks no one is looking? 2) Whine and beg her parents for them? 3) Wait a few more weeks until her allowance catches up and she has enough money to buy them? 4) Ask her parents for extra jobs to earn the money she needs?" As you read the choices, students line up behind the sheet related to the choice they like best. Students may change lines as you give more options. But at the end, they need to choose a line and be able to tell why they made that choice. There don't always have to be clear "right" and "wrong" choices. You might discuss which responses most children chose, and why.

▲ **"RESPONSIBILITY" Word Game.** Hand out a sheet with the word "responsibility" spelled out vertically, one letter per line. Have students fill in the blanks with words related to the idea of being responsible, or with names of characters or words from book titles, that start with each letter in the word. See the blank form and sample answers example on page 14.

▲ **Crossword Puzzle.** p. 15.

▲ **Word Search.** p. 16.

Miscellaneous Activities

Try these activities to help students understand the concepts and practice of responsibility.

▲ **Responsibility Reports.** Invite students to present reports on other books they've read, or TV shows or movies they've seen, that have something to say about responsibility.

▲ **Classroom Responsibilities.** Create a "classroom responsibilities" box with cards in it indicating, with words or pictures, important things that must be done to keep things running smoothly. For example, a card might show someone cleaning the chalk or white board, feeding the class hamster or sweeping the craft area. Choose students each day to draw cards from the box, and then count on them to carry out the tasks responsibly. Perhaps giving students a chance to take on a responsibility could be a reward for positive behavior in the classroom.

▲ **"Catch & Tell."** Challenge students to "catch" each other being responsible, and to tell the teacher about it! Add the name of each student caught behaving responsibly to a list on the board headed, "Catch & Tell: These students were caught being responsible this week." This activity could also be used for other qualities presented throughout this book, by simply changing the heading on the board.

▲ **Venn Diagram.** Choose one of these pairs of characters from the listed books: Angel (*Angel in Charge*) and Ramona (*Ramona Forever*), Marvin (*Marvin Redpost: Alone in his Teacher's House*) and Sam (*The Big Deal*), Jamie (*Jamie's Turn*) and Cecil (*Cecil's Story*). Compare the characters and their situations using a Venn diagram like the example below.

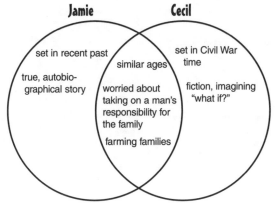

Venn Diagram Sample

▲ **"How Would You Feel If…?"** Help students anticipate how their actions might affect others by asking them to answer "How would you feel if…" questions. Start with examples from the books. You might ask, "How did Songololo feel when Gogo bought him the red shoes?" or "How did Adam (*Duck Boy*) feel when he saw the ducklings swimming with their parents?" Or "How did Maizie feel when Grace hurt herself and Pa couldn't be roused to help?" Move on to examples related to events in the classroom, like "How would you feel if someone kept interrupting you when you tried to talk?" Finally, let students pose "How would you feel if…" questions from their own experience. You can make this game less pointed and personal by writing the questions on cards and having students draw them randomly for response.

Responsibility Word Game

Directions: Fill in each blank with a word that starts with that letter and relates to the idea of responsibility. You may choose to use names of characters or words from responsibility titles you've read, or simply words that relate to the trait. Here's an example to help get you started:

R <u>**Responsibility, Redpost, Ramona, Ross, results, reward**</u>

R _____

E _____

S _____

P _____

O _____

N _____

S _____

I _____

B _____

L _____

E _____

Responsibility Crossword

Directions: Fill in the answers to the crossword using the word bank below.

Across

2. You must accept the _____ of your actions.

3. A _____ person thinks about how his choices will affect other people.

5. Your actions may earn you either rewards or _____.

7. When you make a ____ to someone, you must keep it.

9. When you are responsible, people trust you and _____ on you.

10. A responsible person thinks about how his choices will _____ other people.

11. Part of being responsible is being able to _____ ahead to the possible outcome of your actions.

Down

1. A _____ is an important job or something that someone is counting on you to do.

4. It's important to _____ your mistakes when you make them.

6. A responsible person doesn't make _____ when his decisions turn out badly.

8. When you behave responsibly, you may earn a _____.

Word Bank

admit	consequences	excuses	punishment	responsible	think
affect	count	promise	responsibility	reward	

Responsibility Word Search

Directions: Find and circle the words listed in the word bank below. They may read up, down, across or diagonally.

```
R  B  S  M  W  P  W  Z  W  J  T  X  I  B  B
W  E  L  B  I  S  N  O  P  S  E  R  Y  R  G
J  E  S  I  M  O  R  P  O  V  I  G  R  G  T
G  W  B  P  I  P  S  P  X  H  G  L  K  I  M
N  U  N  P  O  U  I  V  U  O  T  D  G  K  H
H  H  Q  E  C  N  E  U  Q  E  S  N  O  C  L
E  D  B  G  H  I  S  T  L  U  S  E  R  A  W
Y  Y  R  T  T  S  W  I  P  P  Z  P  B  G  B
E  S  U  A  C  H  M  R  B  E  H  E  Q  D  Z
Q  W  Q  B  W  M  I  Y  V  I  C  D  D  T  E
E  X  C  U  S  E  S  N  O  S  L  C  W  M  F
W  P  J  V  N  N  R  V  K  W  J  I  A  O  G
E  F  F  E  C  T  E  O  P  N  W  L  T  D  W
O  Y  P  K  O  M  L  L  X  L  B  L  P  Y  Q
```

Word Bank				
accept	consequence	excuses	responsibility	reward
blame	depend	promise	responsible	think
cause	effect	punishment	results	

2 Respect

Respectful people see all people as valuable and important, not only for what they are, but for what they can be. They treat others the way they want to be treated, and show others courtesy and dignity. They appreciate people who are different from them. They understand that rules meant to protect people's rights, their belongings and the world they share must be obeyed. Respectful people show special courtesy and honor to others who are older or in positions of authority. Protecting your own rights and understanding your own value are important parts of being a respectful person.

You act *respectfully* when you:

- speak politely to your parents.

- take good care of the game you borrowed from your friend.

- obey your teacher in the classroom.

- choose not to tease someone because you might hurt his or her feelings.

- wear a helmet and use proper hand signals when you ride your bike.

- give up your chair to an older person in the doctor's waiting room or on the bus.

- listen carefully to someone else's opinion, even if you disagree.

■ *Be Good to Eddie Lee* by Virginia Fleming. Philomel Books, 1993. K–4. When Christy's neighbor invites her to explore the woods with him, Eddie Lee, a Down's syndrome boy from across the street, follows them. Christy learns something about each boy, and makes a new friend.

■ *Beauty and the Beast* retold by Marianna Mayer. Seastar Publications, 2000. 1–5. Beauty's regard for her father and fairness to the frightening Beast allow her to see the good in the Beast and to free him from his magical spell.

■ *The Bill of Rights* by Warren Coleman. Children's Press, 1987. 2–5. This New True Book explains how and why the bill of Rights was added to the Constitution, and briefly describes each amendment. It stresses the importance of respecting the value of each person, and of laws that protect individual rights.

■ *The Blind Men and the Elephant* by Karen Backstein. Econo-Clad, 1999. 1–2. In this classic tale, six blind men reach different conclusions about the nature of an elephant, from touching different parts of the animal. Only by understanding different points of view can they learn the whole truth.

■ *Bridge to Terabithia* by Katherine Paterson. Econo-Clad, 1999. 4–5. The friendship between two misfits, and the magic of the secret kingdom they create, free both to value themselves, their special gifts, and each other. This Newbery Award Book conveys the sacredness of friendship, imagination, and being yourself.

■ *Brother Eagle, Sister Sky* by Susan Jeffers. Dial Books, 1991. K–5. Chief Seattle's response to the government's request to buy the lands of the Northwest Nations eloquently sets forth the Native American respect for the sacredness of the land and all life on it.

■ *The Butter Battle Book* by Dr. Seuss. Random House, 1984. K–5. The Yooks and the Zooks are brought to the brink of all-out war because they can't tolerate the smallest of differences in their customs.

■ *The Cay* by Theodore Taylor. Avon, 1991. 4–5. During World War II, Phillip finds himself blinded and marooned on a remote island with Timothy, an old West Indian man. His mother has taught him to dislike and mistrust black people, yet he is totally dependent on Timothy. The two develop a deep bond that is timeless and touching. This book won six major awards.

■ *Chester's Way* by Kevin Henkes. Greenwillow Books, 1998. K–2. Chester and his best friend Wilson have their own ways of doing things. When free-spirited Lilly moves into the neighborhood, they shun her company. But Lilly helps them out of a tough spot, and the three decide they have a lot to learn from each other.

■ *Earth Dance* by Joanne Ryder. Henry Holt, Inc., 1996. K–3. This dazzling picture book invites children to identify with, appreciate, and celebrate the earth and every living thing on it.

■ *Just Plain Fancy* by Patricia Polacco. Bantam Books, 1990. K–3. Amish children Naomi and Ruth wish that, just once, they could have something fancy. When the speckled egg they find hatches, they get their wish in the form of a gorgeous peacock. Instead of shunning "Fancy," the elders help Naomi and Ruth learn important lessons about respecting who we are and who we were meant to be.

■ *The Last Dragon* by Susan Miko Nunes. Clarion Books, 1995. K–5. Peter is upset when his parents send him to China Town to get to know his great aunt. But when he spots a dilapidated old dragon in a shop window, things begin to look up. His great aunt gently guides him through an adventure of restoration and discovery that reveals much to value in his cultural heritage.

■ *Mrs. Katz and Tush* by Patricia Polacco. Bantam Books, 1992. K–4. When Larnel finds a litter of kittens, he takes the runt to his elderly neighbor, whom his mother says is lonely. She agrees to keep him if Larnel will help, and a lasting friendship is formed. Larnel learns much from Mrs. Katz as they share their lives, customs and cultures, and he fills an empty place in her heart.

■ *Police Officers* by Paulette Bourgeois. Kids Can Press, 1999. K–3. This title from the In My Neighborhood series uses a loose plot to introduce the role of a local patrol officer, and goes on to explore other law enforcement jobs and roles. It encourages personal safety and respect for public servants.

- *Rosa Parks and the Montgomery Bus Boycott* by Teresa Gelsi. Millbrook Press, 1991. 3–5. Rosa Parks' respect for herself and her people caused her to refuse to give up her bus seat to a white person, setting off the famous 1955 bus boycott, and fueling the Civil Rights Movement.

- *There's a Boy in the Girls' Bathroom* by Louis Sachar. Random House, 1997. 3–5. Bradley is one of those misfits who has resorted to taking pride in being universally disliked and unsuccessful. His fellow students, his teacher, and even his family contribute to his firm conviction that he's a loser. But a new school counselor takes time to listen, respect and offer "no strings attached" acceptance, and Bradley begins to suspect that there's a better person to be found inside. A funny, touching story about an all-too-recognizable character and the magic of simple respect.

- *Veterans Day* by Lynda Sorensen. The Rourke Press, 1994. 1–3. This Rourke's Holiday series title explains the history of Veterans Day, and the importance of honoring those who serve in the armed forces to protect our rights and freedoms.

Other Media

- *Johnny Appleseed* retold by Garrison Keillor. Rabbit Ears Productions, 1991 (videocassette). This quirky telling of the Johnny Appleseed tale gives more depth than most, alluding to his pre-nomadic past and taking him to his peaceful, fanciful death. His reverence for all living things permeates the story.

- *Teaching Peace* by Red Grammer. Smilin' Atcha Music, 1986 (audiocassette). This award-winning cassette includes fun, catchy songs for younger children about self-esteem, praising others, solving problems with words, listening, and celebrating diversity.

- **"The Village of Round and Square Houses"** by Ann Grifalconi, from *Why Mosquitoes Buzz in People's Ears and other Caldecott Classics*. Weston Woods, 1996 (videocassette). K–5. A West African grandmother explains why the villagers live as they do. Spectacular art enhances the tale, which is steeped in respect for elders, traditional customs, and the powers of nature.

Respect Activities

Discussion Prompts

Use these prompts to guide discussions about respect.

- ▲ **Positions of Authority.** Who are the people in positions of authority in your lives? Who are the "elders" that you can learn from? How can you show them special respect?

- ▲ **Respecting Differences.** There are lots of ways that people are different. Give examples from the books in the bibliography (Eddie Lee has a mental disability, Peter Chang is Chinese, etc.). What other differences can you think of? (Students might mention race or culture, language, size, age, jobs or wealth.) How are we alike, in spite of those differences? (Our bodies work the same; our needs, feelings, and wants are similar…) How can we go about learning from someone who is different from us?

  Note: Rap Song from the Teaching Peace *audiocassette would fit here.*

- ▲ **Respect for the Earth.** Johnny Appleseed showed respect for all living things by planting trees, befriending the animals and the pioneers, not hunting or eating meat and sharing news. How can you show respect for the earth and its creatures?

Games

Use these games when students need a change of pace or a lighthearted break from the work of the day.

Note: Some games and activities from the first chapter could be adapted and used here.

- ▲ **"Shining Stars."** This game gets children up and moving, while showing each other respect by praising their good qualities. Post around the room a large yellow star for each student, using names or photos to identify them. Have students go around the room, writing on each star one thing they like about that person. (*Note: You might remind students that they can also show respect during this process by waiting their turn and not getting in each others' way!*) When finished, hand students their stars. Students will use their stars to complete the "My Shining Qualities" sheet. See master sheet, p. 23. The stars can be put back up in

the classroom, or sent home with students' sheets. *Original concept revised with permission from The National Spiritual Assembly of the Baha'is of the U.S.*

Note: A modified version of this game can be played with K–1 students by taking several stars at a time, and having the class share verbally what they like about each student, while you write. You may want to prompt appropriate responses by providing the first quality for each student.

- ▲ **Crossword Puzzle.** p. 24.
- ▲ **Word Search.** p. 25.

Creative Expressions

Have fun with these creative ways to process concepts from the books on the list.

- ▲ **Dance!** Read *Earth Dance*, and invite willing students to make up dances to perform for the class, based on the book. They might use music available in the classroom, or bring appropriate music from home. The song, "Hooray for the World," from the *Teaching Peace* audiocassette, could be used.

- ▲ **Getting to Know You.** *Chester's Way, The Ugly Duckling, Beauty and the Beast, Be Good to Eddie Lee* and *The Cay* all include a character that others judged or misunderstood at first, then came to know and respect. Have students write or tell about someone they didn't like or understand at first, but then got to know and to appreciate. Review the stories, and choose appropriate, respectful examples to share with the class.

- ▲ **"I Like You Just the Way You Are!"** In *Just Plain Fancy* and *The Ugly Duckling*, unusual eggs contained surprises that didn't fit their surroundings at first, but then helped us learn about valuing others and ourselves as we are. Read one or both stories, while students paint or otherwise decorate plastic craft eggs. After completing the story, invite students to tell about someone who helps them feel respected and valuable, just as they are. You might suggest that students give their decorated eggs as gifts of appreciation to that person.

- ▲ **"Look and Listen" Role-play.** Sort a deck of playing cards to include one card for each student, with equal numbers of red and black cards. Pass out the cards. Gather the "red" students, and tell them that they will be teamed with a "black" student, and will tell that student about their favorite book or television show. They should plan to talk for several minutes. Call the "black" students together, and instruct them to respond to their "red" partner's conversation by looking around the room, shifting from foot to foot, humming, glancing at the clock or otherwise showing a lack of attention. Match each "red" student with a "black" student, and prompt the "red" students to begin. Let this go on for a couple of minutes, until the "red" students are beginning to feel uncomfortable. Stop the conversations, and call together the "black" students. Tell them that they will switch roles. This time they will tell about their favorite book or TV show. Gather the "red" students, and instruct them to look their partners in the eye and listen attentively as they talk, nodding their agreement as appropriate, and never interrupting. Recombine and start the role-play again. After a couple of minutes, stop the conversations and lead the class in a discussion about what happened, and how each role play felt to the speaker. Stress how we show respect by paying attention and listening carefully when people speak.

▲ **The Blind Students and the Apple Tree.** Read *The Blind Men and the Elephant* with the class. Enjoy a spontaneous group retelling of the story as it might have gone had the blind men gone to see an apple tree, instead of an elephant. Point out that the blind men had to listen carefully to each experience and point of view to get the whole picture.

▲ **Native America.** Provide a dramatic reading of *Brother Eagle, Sister Sky*, using Native American music in the background (You might use a CD entitled *Keepers of the Dream* by Kevin Locke, from Earthbeat Records, 1994). It could be very effective to have a Native American read the story in traditional dress.

Miscellaneous Activities

Try these activities to help students understand the concepts and practice of respect.

▲ **Welcome Visitors.** Read *Police Officer*, and then invite a police officer to visit the class and talk about his or her role in protecting people's rights and safety. Ask how giving and getting respect is important in doing the work of a police officer. Or read *Veterans Day* and invite a veteran of the armed forces, to share ideas about how veterans have helped protect our freedoms and why we should show them special respect. Prepare the class in advance, by discussing how to show respect for guests and what good questions they might ask.

▲ **Book Discussion Groups.** Assign strong, mature readers to two groups. One group will read *The Cay*, and the other *The Bridge to Terabithia*. After they've completed the books, each group should discuss what their book had to say about respect, using these questions:

• Who showed respect in this book? To whom or to what?

• How did the character(s) show respect?

• What did the book show you about respect that you might remember or use in your own life?

Each group should select a spokesperson to present a short book review and summary of the group's discussion to the other group.

Note: We hear every day about our world getting small, and our country is becoming home to a growing number of immigrants from many parts of the globe. With easy travel, instant communications and an increasingly global economy, it is nearly impossible (and not very interesting) to remain isolated from people whose language or cultural traditions are different from our own. Whether it's a need for tolerance across borders, as in The Butter Battle Book, *or a need to share neighborhoods with people of different cultural backgrounds, as in* Mrs. Katz and Tush, *learning to respect and welcome cultural diversity is critical to Americans. These last two activities address these needs. If your community is not yet very ethnically or culturally diverse, the first activity might be a good place to start. If your community is experiencing growing diversity, the second activity might be more direct and appropriate. Or try them both, and see what you can learn about respecting differences.*

▲ **"Countries of the World" Research Project.** Divide students into small groups. Have each draw a card with the name of a country on it. You might choose countries and prepare the cards to reflect the nationalities most represented in your school or community. Send the groups to the library to learn all they can about their country. They will report back to the class on the items listed on the "Countries of the World" worksheet. See master, p. 26. After each report, ask if any students' families came from that country.

Note: Students may need help with this activity, especially younger ones. Have appropriate research materials available. Also consider inviting parents to help, one for each group. This is a great chance to welcome parents who are recent immigrants themselves, or strongly connected to their country of origin, as appropriate. Encourage sharing about customs, cultures, and adjustments to American life.

▲ **"We're All Immigrants."** A challenge some schools experience is integrating children of different cultures and backgrounds into their classroom communities—especially recent immigrants. This three-part activity can help develop appreciation for the cultural diversity in our individual and community lives.

1. Read or review *Mrs. Katz and Tush.* Point out how Larnel learned from, and shared with, Mrs. Katz until they became like family to each other, in spite of their different backgrounds. Then explain that this whole country is made up of immigrants. Everyone, including Native Americans, came to North America from somewhere else in the world. Tell students the class will explore their immigrant or Native American roots. The teacher should participate in this exercise as well.

2. Send children home with the "Where Do We Come From?" questionnaire. See master, p. 27. Students are to interview their parents, close relatives or neighbors. The idea is to find experiences that are interesting and relevant to the student. These questions will help students understand that their families and those close to them were also immigrants from somewhere else. Students should bring the completed questionnaires back to class.

3. Collect the forms, and discuss all the different places students' families and friends came from.

Note: You will want to send home, with the forms, notes explaining the purpose of the activity, and inviting adults to share their backgrounds and experiences with the students.

My Shining Qualities

_____

(My Name)

I am a valuable person!

These are the qualities that my classmates appreciate in me:

_____

_____

_____

_____

_____

_____

_____

_____

Respect Crossword

Directions: Fill in the answers to the crossword puzzle using the word bank below.

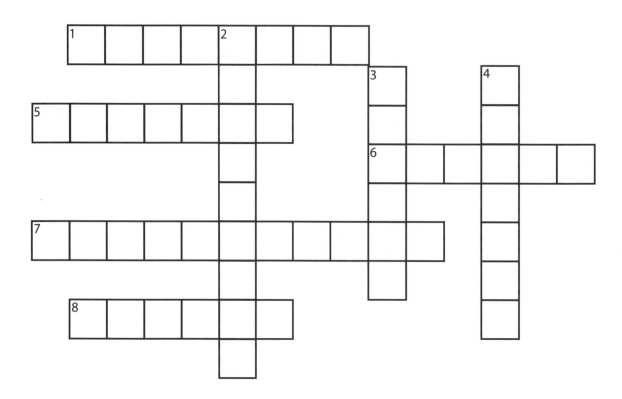

Across

1. All people are important, worthy and _____.

5. Children should obey their _____ and other people in positions of authority.

6. People, animals, and all _____ things deserve our respect.

7. All people have much in common, but our _____ make life more interesting.

8. It is everyone's job to protect the _____ of all people.

Down

2. Children should respect people in positions of _____.

3. The _____ Rule says to treat others the way you want to be treated.

4. When people want to be alone, they ask you to respect their right to _____.

Word Bank

authority	golden	parents	rights
differences	living	privacy	valuable

Respect Word Search

Directions: Find and circle the words listed in the word bank below. They may read up, down, across or diagonally.

```
D  V  K  O  S  P  Y  S  R  J  B  A  Q  N  F
I  R  I  I  B  R  T  W  H  B  Y  D  E  E  X
F  M  M  U  O  K  I  A  E  F  Z  A  L  T  M
F  Q  P  N  C  V  R  L  Y  T  R  D  I  S  X
E  R  O  V  B  C  O  U  R  T  E  S  Y  I  F
R  H  R  V  A  N  H  V  H  R  I  T  R  L  O
E  A  T  V  G  L  T  Q  L  T  C  N  I  P  E
N  Z  A  I  F  A  U  Y  C  E  H  P  G  R  U
C  B  N  A  Q  E  A  A  P  K  I  J  H  I  Z
E  G  T  J  L  F  S  S  B  M  E  Z  T  V  D
S  R  E  H  C  A  E  T  Z  L  P  S  S  A  P
Q  S  T  N  E  R  A  X  E  Z  E  M  P  C  V
S  T  N  E  R  A  P  F  S  E  L  U  R  Y  Z
W  W  X  J  B  N  F  U  Q  S  M  D  U  V  Z
```

Word Bank

authority	dignity	honor	parents	rules
belongings	Earth	important	privacy	teachers
courtesy	elderly	laws	respect	valuable
differences	esteem	listen	rights	

Countries of the World

Our country to study is: _____

- Find this country on a world map. Be prepared to show the class where it is.

- In the space below, draw a picture of this country's national flag.

- What is the weather like in this country? _____
_____

- What is the name of the capitol city? _____

- Bring to class a picture showing part of this country.

- Bring to class a picture of people from this country.

- What language do most people speak in this country? _____

- How do people greet each other in this language? Be prepared to show and tell the class how you would say "hello" if you lived in this country.

Where Do We Come From?

Student's Name: _____

Interviewee's Name and Relationship to Student: _____

Note to family member or friend: The United States is a country made up almost entirely of immigrants. You or your ancestors came here from some other part of the world. Our country is what it is today because people from so many different places and cultures worked hard and shared their lives and customs with each other. Please help this student learn about your family's Native American or immigrant roots by answering these questions. We hope this will give you a chance to explore, share, and take pride in your own family's heritage. Many American families are of mixed background. Please comment on the major cultures or nationalities that make up your ancestral history, as best you can. Feel free to use the back of the sheet, or to add extra sheets to tell your story.

- Is your family of Native-American background?

- If so, what nation or tribe?

- What members of your family came from this background?

- If you do not have a Native-American heritage, what country or countries did your ancestors come from?

- Do you know how many generations ago your ancestors immigrated to America? If so, please list it here.

- Are you still in touch with relatives in the country or countries of your ancestors? Do you ever visit those places?

- If you know how your first American ancestors made their living, please list it here.

- Are there famous people, either in the US or in other countries, among your ancestors? If so, please mention them briefly here.

- Do you practice traditions from the culture or cultures of your ancestors? If so, please comment about them briefly here.

Thank you for helping us learn about our country!

3 Caring

Caring means feeling kindness for people, animals and the earth, and expressing that feeling through acts of generosity and service. Caring people understand the feelings of others and go out of their way to help them. They are unselfish, and can put the needs of others before their own when it's appropriate. Caring people take good care of themselves and do their very best at the jobs they take on.

You show *caring* when you:

- visit a sick or lonely person to cheer him or her up.

- help your mother make dinner when she comes home tired from work.

- comfort a friend when his or her feelings have been hurt.

- forgive someone who has hurt your feelings.

- play with your cat before having your snack because he's been alone all day.

- pick up the litter you find on your street.

- eat lunch with a new student in your class to help him or her feel welcome.

Caring Resources

- *Abuelita's Heart* by Amy Cordova. Simon & Schuster Books for Young Readers, 1997. 2–4. A little girl visits her Abuelita (grandmother) in her Southwest canyon home. Abuelita cooks her favorite meal, teaches her about medicinal herbs, and shares a secret with her. The lovely artwork and Spanish words interspersed through the text make this a rich picture book experience.

- *All Kinds of Families* by Norma Simon. Albert Whitman & Co.,1987. K–3. Simon tells about many different kinds and combinations of people that make up families, and explores the core of caring and sharing that they have in common.

- *Beethoven Lives Upstairs* by Barbara Nichol. Orchard Books, 1993. 3–5. In Vienna in 1822, Christoph writes letters to his uncle complaining of the chaos caused by the family's new renter, Ludwig van Beethoven. Over time, Christoph comes to understand the lonely, eccentric genius, and to care for him. The letters weave actual incidents from Beethoven's life with fictional characters and events.

- *Bub or the Very Best Thing* by Natalie Babbitt. HarperCollins Publishers, 1994. K–2. The king and queen agree that they want what's best for the prince, but they're not sure what that is. They try, in their own ways, to learn what's best. The answer, it seems, is simpler than they imagined.

- *A Chair for My Mother* by Vera B. Williams. Greenwillow Books, 1982. K–3. A young girl, her mother and grandmother work hard to save money for a comfortable chair, after their belongings are lost in a fire. The book tells of family and community caring, and the resulting strength and happiness. A Caldecott Honor Book.

- *Christopher Reeve: Actor and Activist* by Margaret L. Finn. Chelsea House, 1997. 3–5. Reeve was best known as Superman in the movies, before the 1995 accident that left him a quadriplegic. His knowledge that his family needed him and that he could use his celebrity to help others kept him going, and motivated him to redirect his lifelong social activism into advocating for people with spinal cord injuries.

- *Crow Boy* by Yashima Taro. Econo-Clad, 1999. K–3. Chibe is different from other kids. He is small, doesn't learn easily, and makes faces. The children tease him and call him names, until finally a teacher takes time to get to know him and discovers his knowledge and love of nature. By nurturing Chibe's special gifts, the teacher helps him find his place of honor and dignity. This Caldecott Honor Book is not subtle in its message, but could be used to good effect. See the first Discussion Prompt on p. 31.

- *The Family Under the Bridge* by Natalie Savage Carlson. HarperTrophy, 1989. 3–5. Old homeless Armand loves his carefree, solitary life. But when his shelter under a Paris bridge is taken over by three needy children, his gruff exterior can't hide his soft heart, and a new kind of family begins to take shape. A Newbery Honor Book.

- *The Five-Dog Night* by Eileen Christelow. Clarion, 1993. K–2. Ezra and Old Betty are neighbors who bother and annoy each other. A particularly cold winter causes them to come to appreciate one another as caring friends.

- *The Hundred Dresses* by Eleanor Estes. Econo-Clad, 1999. 2–4. Poor Polish immigrant girl Wanda is teased by the girls when she claims to have 100 dresses at home. Wanda's family moves away to escape intolerance and ridicule, just as her 100 drawings of dress designs explain her claim and win a prize. Her classmates deal with feelings of guilt. Another pointed story about teasing. See the first Discussion Prompt on p. 31.

- *Lucy's Picture* by Nicola Moon. Dial Books for Young Readers, 1994. K–3. Lucy's Grandpa is coming! Her teacher lets her create a collage as a gift for him, but she needs just the right materials. In a surprise twist, we discover that Grandpa is blind, explaining her insistence on textures in her gift. Grandpa declares, "It's the best picture I've ever seen!"

- *Mr. Popper's Penguins* by Richard & Florence Atwater. Little, Brown and Co., 1992. 2–4. In this hilarious Newbery Honor Book, Mr. Popper receives the gift of a penguin from Antarctica, and his family's life is turned upside down. Tucked into the delightful nonsense are great examples of creativity, affection and selfless caring.

- *Mr. Putter and Tabby Walk the Dog* by Cynthia Rylant. Harcourt, Brace & Co., 1994. 1–2. Mr. Putter is glad to help out his neighbor when she hurts her foot. But when he agrees to walk her dog, he discovers that Mrs. Teaberry's "dream dog" is really a nightmare.

- *A River Ran Wild* by Lynne Cherry. Gulliver Green, 1992. K–5. This lovely picture book tells the story of the Nashua River from nearly 7000 years ago until the early '90s, focusing on environmental issues of use, abuse, pollution and clean-up. It features the dedicated efforts of Marion Stoddart to restore the river's health.

- *The Sign of the Beaver* by Elizabeth George Speare. Bantam, 1995. 4–5. When 12-year-old Matt is left to guard the frontier cabin while his father goes back for the rest of the family, he has an accident and is saved and assisted by Indians. Matt and the Indians learn from each other, and develop a bond of caring and friendship that transforms their lives and attitudes. A Newbery Honor Book.

- *Somebody Loves You, Mr. Hatch* by Eileen Spinelli. Aladdin Paperbacks, 1996. K–2. When loner Mr. Hatch receives candy from a secret admirer, feeling loved causes him to get involved with the people in his neighborhood in kind and caring ways.

- *A Symphony of Whales* by Steve Schuch. Harcourt, Brace & Co., 1999. K–5. Glashka and her sled dogs discover thousands of whales trapped by suddenly frozen waters. Her whole village joins forces to keep the whales alive until a Russian ice-breaking vessel can rescue them. Their self-sacrificing care and creative thinking keep the whales alive and lure them to follow the ship back to open waters and safety. A New York Times Best Illustrated Children's Book.

- *Uncle Willie and the Soup Kitchen* by Dyanne DiSalvo-Ryan. Morrow Junior Books, 1991. K–3. A young boy gets a close-up look at community caring in action, when he goes to help at the soup kitchen where his uncle works.

- *Wilfrid Gordon McDonald Partridge* by Mem Fox. Kane/Miller Book Publishers, 1985. K–2. Wilfrid lives next door to an old people's home, and the residents are his friends. When his favorite resident starts losing her memory, Wilfrid sets out to learn what "memory" is and to help her restore it. A touching example of creative caring.

Other Media

- **"The Face in the Lake,"** from *Listen to the Storyteller: A Trio of Musical Tales from Around the World* by Kristen Balouch, music by Wynton Marsalis, et al. Viking: Penguin, 1998 (book and CD). In this musical tale, the beautiful maiden of spring is imprisoned by her cruel brother winter, freezing the world until the power of genuine, unselfish love releases her.

- **"Mufaro's Beautiful Daughters"** by John Steptoe, from *Why Mosquitoes Buzz in People's Ears and other Caldecott Classics.* Weston Woods, 1996 (videocassette). K–5. In this African tale, the king announces he's looking for a wife. Mufaro is proud to send both his daughters as candidates. But in approaching the prospect of becoming queen, the two girls' true natures are revealed.

Caring Activities

Discussion Prompts

Use these starting points to guide discussions about caring.

▲ **Teasing and Ridicule.** Both *Crow Boy* and *The Hundred Dresses* are pointed stories about teasing and ridicule. While they may be heavy-handed for general use, a teacher, counselor or parents could use either effectively with an individual student or group of students in cases where cruel teasing is an issue. The teacher or parent might ask students why children teased the child in the book, and how they thought it made the child feel. Next they could move closer to reality by asking students if they had ever been teased that way, or if they'd ever teased another child that way. Finally, they could proceed to address the specific situation. It would be important to help students find ways to apologize and make amends, so the situation can be resolved with everyone feeling cared for and accepted.

▲ **Taking Care.** Part of caring is "taking care of" something or someone. Share examples from the stories; like Abuelita (*Abuelita's Heart*) feeding her granddaughter dinner, Mr. Putter (*Mr. Putter and Tabby Walk the Dog*) walking Mr. Teaberry's dog or Saknis and Attean (*Sign of the Beaver*) tending Matt after his bee stings. Have the class brainstorm things they could do to help take care of:

- a baby brother
- a pet turtle
- an elderly neighbor
- a sick friend.

▲ **"I Know You Really Care."** In *The Five-Dog Night*, Ezra and Old Betty scold and fuss at each other. How do we know that they care for each other? Are there people in your life who seem to grumble and fight, when you know they really care for each other? How do they show their caring?

Note: You might set an appropriate tone by offering the example that siblings often argue, even though they really love each other.

▲ **Selflessness.** Share examples of selfless or self-sacrificing service from the books. For example, in *A Symphony of Whales*, Glashka's entire community left their cozy village to help keep the whales alive, and Glashka gave the whales part of her own ration of food. And in *Mufaro's Beautiful Daughters*, Nyasha gives a hungry boy the yam she brought for her own lunch. Prompt discussion with these questions.

• Can you think of a time when someone helped you by putting your needs before his or her own?

• Can you think of a time when you gave away something important to you or did something that was difficult or unpleasant for you, just because you cared for someone else?

• Think of a person that you care about very much. What could you do to show that person that you care as much about him or her as you do about yourself?

Games

Use these games when students need a change of pace or a break from the work of the day.

Note: Some games and activities from the first chapter could be adapted and used here.

▲ **Word Search.** p. 34.

▲ **"How Does it Feel?"** Compassion is an important part of caring. Students with no sense of others' feelings have trouble experiencing and expressing kindness and service. This game gives students a small experience of the problems created by a disability. It may help them feel more sensitive to people with real disabilities and think of ways to be of service. Divide the class into four groups. Blindfold one group, have a second group use earplugs, wrap scarves around the mouths of a third group to remind them not to speak, and confine the fourth group to chairs to symbolize wheelchairs. Go about normal classroom activities for 30 to 60 minutes, including activities that challenge limits to sight, hearing, speech and mobility. Encourage students to find ways to ask for help and to offer help. Process the experience by discussing how students felt, and by coming up with ways they might be more helpful in the future to people with real disabilities.

Note: You might send a note home to parents in advance of this activity, explaining its purpose and encouraging follow-up discussion at home.

▲ **"Kindness Tag."** Prepare a box containing slips of paper with the names of your students, one name per slip. To begin, call on a student to draw a name randomly from the box. That student must look for an opportunity to do or say something kind to the person named on the slip. Upon accomplishing the task, the kind student says, "Tag, You're It!" The new "It" goes to the box and draws another name, and the game continues until each student in the class has received and extended a kindness. This game might last a day or a week, as other activities continue, depending on the emphasis you give it and the creativity of your students. Or try this variation, if you want to add some subtlety and depth to the game for older students: Have students draw names for "secret pals," like you would for a "secret Santa" activity in December. Give them a week to find opportunities to do or say kind things to or about their secret pal, without being obvious about it. Have students try to guess who their secret pal is at the end of the week, and say thanks.

Creative Expressions

Have fun with these creative ways to process concepts from the books on the list.

▲ **Caring Collage.** Review the Christopher Reeve biography and/or *A River Ran Wild*, and talk about how Reeve and Stoddart showed their caring through dedicated service to others. Have students choose a person who has dedicated his/her life to helping others. You might provide a list of people appropriate to your local or national scene to get them started, and allow them to choose a name or come up with someone else on their own. Students will then create a collage or poster showing the actions and achievements of that person.

▲ **Random Acts of Kindness.** Have students share brief stories about acts of kindness they have done or received. Write up the anecdotes, have students illustrate the pages and compile them into a book for the classroom library.

▲ **"Silly Scenarios."** This activity encourages students to have fun and be creative while figuring out ways to provide help, kindness and caring. In *Mr. Popper's Penguins*, the Popper family goes to great lengths to meet the needs of the penguins in their warm home and climate. They drill holes in the refrigerator for air and move the penguins inside, build an ice castle in the basement, and order canned shrimp by the case. Invite students to form groups and create stories, skits or songs expressing ways they might meet the needs of their animal guests in one of the following scenarios.

- A dolphin in your desert home.
- A tropical iguana in Alaska.
- A camel in New York City.

Have each group share its story, skit or song with the rest of the class.

▲ **Jars of Kindness.** In *A Chair for My Mother*, the family keeps a jar for coins to buy a comfortable chair as a gift for each other. Have students bring jars from home and decorate them with paint, glitter, strips of colored paper, etc. Students will take the jars home to save money to buy small gifts of kindness for people they care about.

▲ **Personal Gifts.** Read *Lucy's Picture*. Talk about what made Lucy's gift for her grandfather so appropriate. Help children think of someone they know with a disability (is there someone in the school community they might consider?). Have students create an appropriate small gift for that person. For example, they might copy and decorate a poem for a person who is hearing-impaired; create or decorate a simple musical instrument (inexpensive wood instruments can be found in educational supply stores), for a person who is sight-impaired; or put together a small, hand-held game like "cat's cradle" for a person with difficulty moving around. Encourage them to deliver their gifts.

Miscellaneous Activities

Try these activities to help students understand the concepts and practice of caring.

▲ **Field Trip: Nursing Home.** Read *Wilfrid Gordon McDonald Partridge*, and then arrange a field trip to a nursing home. Help students think of questions to ask the residents about their lives, their families or their favorite memories. As a class, prepare to offer some service to the residents, like reading a story or poem, singing a song or taking treats. As a teacher, be alert for chances to model small acts of kindness like opening doors, friendly greetings, or fetching something a resident can't reach. This is a chance to demonstrate and practice both respect and caring.

▲ **Field Trip: Food Bank/Homeless Shelter.** Read *Uncle Willy and the Soup Kitchen*, and arrange a visit to a food bank, soup kitchen or homeless shelter. At a food bank, students might be able to actually help stock shelves, take inventory or assist in some other way. Again, prepare students with good questions to ask, and look for opportunities to show caring and respect. This would also be a good follow-up activity after reading *The Family Under the Bridge.*

▲ **The Arithmetic of Caring.** Caring spreads rapidly, like a happy version of the flu! Read *Somebody Loves You, Mr. Hatch.* Talk about how when Mr. Hatch felt loved he was eager to do kind, generous things for others. When he didn't, he kept to himself. Count with the class the number of people Mr. Hatch helped and had fun with in the story. Now work with the class to figure out these problems:

• If your teacher shows caring by doing something kind for one student this week, that student does something kind for another student the next week, and so on throughout the class, how many weeks would it take for every student in the class to experience caring? (In a class of 25 students and a teacher, it would take 25 weeks.)

• If your teacher feels cared about, he or she might show special kindness to two students this week. Next week, both the teacher and those two students might pass on that kindness to two other students each, and so on. At that rate, how many weeks would it take for every student in the class to experience caring? (In the same class of 25 students, it would take less than three weeks!) You might either chart the weeks, as in the example below, or actually call up students to the front of the room, by alphabetical or seating order so as not to show preference or leave anyone out, to demonstrate the rapid spread of caring by week. With older students, this makes an easy segue into a math lesson about arithmetic versus geometric progression. And it

clearly shows how, with a little effort, a class could begin to feel like a caring community in a very short time.

▲ **Community Service Project.** Lead the class in a discussion about a service project to take on together. Find something appropriate to your school or community. These examples might help get ideas flowing:

• Plant a tree or paint benches at a park near the school.

• Collect canned goods for a food bank.

• Collect supplies for an animal shelter.

Research the group's favorite ideas to find one that is manageable. Remember to approach the people you wish to serve with respect and caring. Make a plan for carrying out the project, and seek appropriate support from the school, parents, etc. Complete your project, and write it up for the local newspaper.

▲ **Book Discussion Groups.** Assign older readers to two groups. One group will read *The Sign of the Beaver,* and the other *The Family Under the Bridge.* After reading the books, each group should discuss what their book had to say about caring, using these questions:

• How did individuals show caring in this book? How did the book illustrate caring in families and in communities?

• What was surprising to you about the caring relationships shown in the book? (We don't often see white settlers and Indians portrayed as caring friends, nor do we think of homeless people or gypsies as caring families and communities.)

• What did you learn about caring that might help you in your own life?

Each group should select a spokesperson to give a short book review and summary of the group's discussion to the other group.

Week 1	Week 2	Week 3
♀♀♀	♀♀♀	♀♀♀
	♀♀ ♀♀ ♀♀	♀♀ ♀♀ ♀♀
		♀♀ ♀♀ ♀♀ ♀♀ ♀♀ ♀♀ ♀♀ ♀♀

Caring Chart Example

Caring Word Search

Directions: Find and circle the words listed in the word bank below. They may read up, down, across or diagonally.

```
S  S  E  N  E  V  I  G  R  O  F  Y  T  F  X
S  C  H  E  L  P  I  N  G  Y  T  H  E  Y  R
E  A  R  I  R  I  N  L  E  I  F  C  S  S  S
N  R  V  E  T  A  P  Y  N  R  I  M  D  S  E
S  I  C  C  A  H  Z  U  E  V  B  B  E  I  K
S  N  T  F  M  T  M  O  R  H  D  N  E  F  Q
E  G  L  S  H  M  I  E  O  I  D  N  N  T  S
L  I  A  A  O  T  S  V  S  N  S  Y  B  G  A
F  V  G  C  N  Y  L  P  I  Y  U  W  M  P  P
L  I  O  R  L  Y  W  K  T  T  I  Y  B  D  T
E  N  U  I  J  O  T  N  Y  Q  Y  W  O  Q  S
S  G  M  F  I  K  S  E  J  H  U  Y  D  J  D
G  A  O  I  N  O  W  J  W  E  X  E  U  C  E
F  O  T  C  E  R  C  H  F  F  Y  W  C  O  P
W  N  F  E  R  W  Q  Y  F  P  R  A  C  T  F
```

Word Bank

caring	family	giving	needs	service
community	forgiveness	helping	sacrifice	
creativity	generosity	kindness	selflessness	

4 Honesty

Honesty is more than just telling the truth. It's about earning people's trust by keeping your promises, and by refusing to lie, cheat or steal. An honest person admits mistakes and doesn't exaggerate to impress people or take credit for the work of others. His actions match his words, and he listens to his conscience to know what's right and wrong.

You show *honesty* when you:

- return the money when you're given too much change at the store.

- refuse to help your friend cheat on a test at school.

- admit to your parents that you broke the window with your ball.

- keep your friend's secret after promising to do so.

- admit to yourself that you were not kind to your brother or sister, and try to do better.

- find a tactful way to tell the truth when your friend asks if you like his or her new clothes and you don't.

- **"And to Think That I Saw It on Mulberry Street"** by Dr. Seuss. From *Six by Seuss*. Random House, 1997. K–5. Knowing his father always asks what he saw on the way home from school, Marco spends the walk embellishing the sights as only a Dr. Seuss character could! A delightful look at the magic of imagination, and the wisdom of being able to distinguish it from reality.

- *A Big Fat Enormous Lie* by Marjorie Weinman Sharmat. Dutton, 1993. K–2. When a little boy lies to his father, his conscience turns the lie into a monster that keeps getting bigger. The only way to get rid of the monster is to own up and tell the truth.

- *The Cold and Hot Winter* by Johanna Hurwitz. Apple, 1993. 2–5. Bolivia is making a return visit to liven up winter vacation for neighborhood friends Rory and Derek. Their fun takes an unexpected turn when things start to turn up missing, and the friendships are tested by accusations of lies, cheating and stealing. A good example of the fragility of trust once lost, the insidious nature of suspicion, and the power of second chances.

- *A Day's Work* by Eve Bunting. Clarion Books, 1994. K–3. Francisco is proud when he helps his grandfather, who doesn't speak English, get a gardening job by saying they are gardeners. But their mistakes on the job expose the lie. Grandfather insists on making it right and refuses pay until he has done so, teaching Francisco an important lesson and winning his new employer's trust.

- *The Empty Pot* by Demi. Henry Holt, 1996. K–3. The Emperor must choose a successor. He gives each child in the land a flower seed, and announces that the child who shows him his best flower the next year will be the new Emperor. The results are surprising, and the only honest child in the land wins the prize.

- *The Honest-to-Goodness Truth* by Patricia McKissack. Atheneum, 2000. K–3. Libby knows it's right to tell the truth and never lie. So why does she get in so much trouble when she does just that? In this appealing, beautifully illustrated picture book, Libby learns some lessons about when and how to tell the truth, and which truths are hers to tell.

- *Honest Tulio* by John Himmelman. Bridge Water Books, 1997. K–2. Tulio's dream is to have his own stall in the market. When he pursues a man who dropped a coin, in order to return it, his fame as an honest man spreads and he secures the means to realize his dream. A fun, progressive story.

- *Inspirations: Stories About Woman Artists* by Leslie Sills. Albert Whitman & Company, 1989. 4–5. Sills explores the lives and work of four American artists—Georgia O'Keeffe, Frida Kahlo, Alice Neel and Faith Ringgold. While these women came from different backgrounds and developed different styles, they all remained true to their unique artistic visions, and depicted their feelings, their struggles and the world around them with great honesty.

- *Ivan the Great* by Isabel Langis Cusack. Thomas Y. Crowell, 1978. 1–3. Robbie gets a talking parrot named Ivan for his birthday. When Robbie discovers that Ivan actually converses with him, confusion sets in. Robbie is punished for lies he didn't tell, and rewarded when he does lie. Ivan convinces Robbie to be true to himself, and the rest will sort itself out.

- *Jamaica's Find* by Juanita Havill. Econo-Clad, 1999. K–2. Jamaica finds a sock and a stuffed dog at the park. She turns in the sock, but takes the dog home. When her parents and her conscience convince her to return the dog, she feels better about herself and makes a new friend as well.

- *The Pied Piper of Hamelin* retold by Sara and Stephen Corrin. Harcourt Brace Jovanovich, 1989. K–5. A compelling version of this classic tale in which a greedy village pays the terrible price of the loss of its children for breaking their promise. A concluding essay on possible origins of the story offers a history tie-in.

- *Sam, Bangs & Moonshine* by Evaline Ness. Econo-Clad, 1999. K–5. Samantha has a habit of telling stories—"Moonshine," her father calls it. Mostly, they're harmless imagination. But one day they put her friend's and her cat's lives at risk, and she is forced to learn the difference between reality and "moonshine."

- *The Skull of Truth* by Bruce Coville. Harcourt Brace & Company, 1997. 3–5. Charlie, who is known as a liar, is in deep trouble. His opposition to a plan to drain his beloved swamp to build an industrial park is making him the victim of bullies. And his sudden and mysterious possession of the skull of truth, which prevents him from lying, causes him more problems than the lies did! A pleasantly creepy and satisfying look at the power, forms and faces of truth.

- **The Stories Julian Tells** by Ann Cameron. Econo-Clad, 1999. K–2. Julian has a knack for wishful thinking, imaginative storytelling, and just plain fibbing. This book of chapter-length stories is filled with humor, mischief, consequences and caring parenting. Later Julian stories would also work here.

- **The Truthful Harp** by Lloyd Alexander. Holt, Rinehart and Winston, 1967. 2–5. King Fflewddur wants to be a bard. When the Chief Bard gives him a magic harp to test his worthiness, the results are mixed – his deeds are laudable, but his fancies get out of control and his words are less than truthful. A good look at imagination, "kind lies," and the significance of deeds over words.

- **Undercover Tailback** by Matt Christopher. Little, Brown and Company, 1992. 3–5. Because of his history of lying, nobody believes Parker when he reports a suspicious character in the coach's office. But games start going wrong, and Parker has a mystery to solve and his credibility to recover. A solid story about the consequences of lying and cheating, mixed with lots of Matt Christopher play-by-play action for sports fans.

- **Your Move, J.P.!** by Lois Lowry. Yearling Books, 1990. 3–5. Twelve-year-old J.P. is smart, has a great memory, and is chess champ. But none of that helps him when new student Angela enters the room and he falls hopelessly, stupidly in love. All he cares about is impressing her, and in the process, he's caught up in a web of almost-accidental lies. Funny and believable.

Other Media

- **The Emperor's New Clothes: An All-Star Retelling of the Classic Fairy Tale.** Harcourt Brace & Company, 1998 (book and CD). K–5. This hilarious version of the famous tale was created as a benefit for the Starbright Foundation. Illustrations and performances are sure to make students giggle, as they hear the satisfying story of foolish ego and of honesty rewarded.

- **Pecos Bill** retold by Brian Gleeson. Rabbit Ears Productions, 1988 (videocassette). K–5. Robin Williams narrates this knee-slapping version of the tales about Pecos Bill as he rides his trusty cougar mount, cracks his snake whip, and carves out the Grand Canyon riding a wild tornado. The tape offers a good chance to talk about truth, lies, imagination and tall tales.

Honesty Activities

Discussion Prompts

Use these starting points to guide discussions about honesty.

▲ **Shades of Meaning.** Watch *Pecos Bill* or read *And to Think that I Saw it on Mulberry Street*, and explore the relationship between imagination, storytelling and truth.

• Are these stories true? (Did Pecos Bill carve out the Grand Canyon while riding a tornado? Did Marco really see an elephant pulling a brass band?)

• Are they lies?

• What are they?

Talk about the human imagination, and the wonderful things it produces for us, like art, music and stories. Discuss how they enrich our lives, and often carry their own truth. Point out that stories and tall tales are usually harmless and often useful. They help us learn and understand things in a new way. They are only bad or harmful if we convince ourselves or others that they are literally true.

▲ **Honesty Rewards.** In several of the stories (*The Empty Pot, The Emperor's New Clothes, Jamaica's Find, A Day's Work*), characters are rewarded for their honesty. Review specific examples from these stories. Then consider these questions:

• Have you ever been rewarded for doing the honest thing? Tell us about it.

• Is honest behavior always rewarded by others?

• Why is it important to be honest, even when it does not bring outward rewards?

▲ **Negative Consequences.** In other stories from the bibliography (*Undercover Tailback, Ivan the Great, The Skull of Truth, Sam, Bangs & Moonshine, The Cold and Hot Winter*) characters are not trusted or believed because they have a reputation for lying. Review examples from these stories. Then explore these questions:

• How did these characters lose the trust of the people around them?

• Are there people you don't trust because they've lied to you? (Don't name names.)

• How did (or could) these characters win back the trust of those around them?

▲ **Lies and More Lies.** In *Ivan the Great*, Ivan tells Robby that there are many different kinds of lies. Talk about the kinds of lies listed below. Share, or have students find, examples of each from the stories. Examples can be found in many of the stories; one source has been given for each.

• Fib (*A Day's Work*)

• Whopper (*The Skull of Truth*)

• Little white lie (*The Truthful Harp*)

• "Saving face" (*Ivan the Great*)

• Exaggeration (*Undercover Tailback*)

• Rationalization (*Ivan the Great*)

• Fantasizing (*Sam, Bangs & Moonshine*)

• Silent lie (*Your Move, J.P.!*)

• Gossip (*Undercover Tailback*)

• Broken promise (*The Pied Piper*)

Explore with students why people tell lies. Is it always wrong to lie? Are there any "good" lies? Ivan tells Robby that his first real lie was when he lied to himself, and that the most important thing is to be honest with yourself, no matter what other people believe. What do you think he means? Is he right?

▲ **A World of Honesty.** What other ways are there to be honest, besides not telling lies? Share examples from the stories, and point out positive examples from classroom experience. Brainstorm about what would be the best thing about a world in which everyone was honest.

Games

Use these games when students need a change of pace or a break from the work of the day. *Note: Some games and activities from the first chapter could be adapted and used here.*

▲ **Crossword Puzzle.** p. 41.

▲ **The Gossip Game.** Gossip is a particular kind of lie that is usually meant to make the person starting the gossip feel important, or to hurt the feelings of the person it's about. Play this version of the telephone game to demonstrate how, even if the initial piece of gossip is factually accurate, it quickly becomes distorted and untrue. Have students sit in a circle. Whisper to the first student a message about a made-up person. Be sure not to use the name of anyone in the class or the school community. You might try something like this: "I heard that Jerome didn't do his homework because his dog died, so he got in trouble. Pass it on." Students should whisper this around the circle, one time only—no repeats. When the message gets back to the beginning of the circle, have the last student say it out loud. By this time, it will probably be quite different from the original message. Process the experience by discussing why it's important not to start or spread gossip.

▲ **"Where Do You Stand?"** from Chapter 1. Use the directions in Chapter 1, substituting scenarios about honesty. For example, you might say, "Alonzo takes his little sister to the store. After leaving, he discovers that she has a candy bar that they didn't pay for. Should he 1) Scold her and go on home? 2) Return to the store to explain and pay for the candy? 3) Say nothing and go home, because it's only one candy bar and the store won't miss it? 4) Laugh and ask her for a bite?

▲ **"Oh, What a Tangled Web…."** This can be fun and creative while illustrating how complicated we make our lives when we begin to lie. However, the teacher has to stay alert to keep this one moving! It can't be scripted, because each new prompt builds on the spontaneous response of the last student to speak. The teacher begins by setting up a scenario. For example, "School has just gotten out, and Jennifer catches up with Alice to ask her to play on the playground. Alice doesn't want to play with Jennifer, so she lies and says, 'I can't because…'" Point to a student to provide an excuse. If the student says, "I promised Noreen that I'd go to her house after school," the teacher might continue with "But just then Noreen's mom drives up, and Noreen runs out and gets in the car without even looking at Alice. Alice has to think fast. She says, 'What I mean is that…'" Look for a volunteer to provide the next excuse. Follow the scenario through several lies, if possible, leading Alice into a situation in which she has to remember what lie she told to whom, so as not to trip herself up further. For example, a student might have Alice say that she's going to Noreen's the next day, so she has to go right home and practice piano today. Then you might have Jennifer telling Noreen at school the next day that she heard Alice was going to her house that afternoon, etc. Ask students if they've ever gotten themselves into

such a fix by telling lies. Point out that it makes life very complicated when you tell one lie, and then try to cover it with another lie. You're very likely to get caught in such a web of lies, and it's much easier to just tell the truth in the first place. You might also point out that if you think carefully and act responsibly in the first place, you're less likely to be tempted to lie to get yourself out of trouble!

Creative Expressions

Have fun with these creative ways to process concepts from the books on the list.

▲ **Unique Visions.** Review *Inspirations: Stories About Women Artists.* Point out that these four women developed very different styles, but each was true to her own artistic vision, and expressed her feelings and ideas honestly in her artwork. Have all students create a picture of the same item, perhaps a tree visible from a classroom window. Offer options of black and white drawings, color paintings or mixed material collages. Tell students not to sign their pictures. Post the pictures around the classroom, and discuss how they are similar and different. Emphasize that each student artist, seeing the same image, expressed it in a way that was honest and unique to his or her vision.

▲ **Tall Tales.** Have students make up, write or record on audiocassette, and illustrate their own "tall tale" to explain something in human nature or in the physical world. You might want to have a list of possible subjects, like "How the stars came to be in the sky," or "Why a smile means the same thing everywhere." Students should share their tales with the class.

▲ **Honesty in Advertising.** Invite older students to study TV commercials to see how they make unfounded claims or stretch the truth to make you want to buy their product. Team up students to write and perform an honest commercial for one of these products:

• A snack food

• Bath soap

• Sport shoes

• A bicycle.

▲ **Listen to Your Conscience.** In *A Big Fat Enormous Lie,* a little boy's conscience causes his lie to his father to turn into a huge monster. Only by telling the truth is he able to get rid of the monster. Talk about what the word "conscience" means. Ask students for their ideas and then look it up in a dictionary. After the discussion, have each student create a picture, poem or song about listening to his or her conscience.

Miscellaneous Activities

Try these activities to help students understand the concepts and practice of caring.

▲ **Adopt a "Second Chance Policy" in the Classroom.** Most of us do something less than honest now and then, and we want to help each other learn to be more honest and truthful. So if someone makes a mistake and does something dishonest, he can make up for it. He can go back to the person affected by his action, call on the "Second Chance Policy," admit his mistake, apologize, and try to make it right. By adopting an official class policy, each student buys into the agreement to ask for a second chance when appropriate, and to forgive a fellow student when asked.

▲ **Victims of Truth-telling.** Review *The Honest-to-Goodness Truth* with the class. Part of honesty is being frank and open with your real feelings and opinions. But being kind and caring is as important as being honest. That's where tact comes in. Write challenging scenarios on index cards. Have students draw cards and respond in an honest, tactful way. Cards might read as follows: "Your friend got a new haircut, and wants to know if you like it. You don't!" or "A classmate is upset about a bad grade on a test. You got an 'A,' and you don't know how to answer when he says it was a really hard test, and asks how you did." You may need to model an appropriate answer ("You always look nice, but I think I like your hair better when it's longer.") Encourage students to help each other—this is hard! Have fun with it. There are no "right" answers. Point out that adults have trouble with this, too. But it's important to try to be truthful without being cruel.

▲ **Magic Show!** Invite a magician to perform for your class. Enjoy the show, and then discuss with the magician how he creates his or her illusions. The job of a magician is to "trick" us, and most magicians stay true to themselves and their profession by keeping the secrets of their trade. Is this dishonest?

▲ **Caught Being Honest.** Write "honesty" on the board. Watch for examples of honest behavior among students, and have students watch each other. Each time someone sees an example of honest behavior, color one letter of the word. When all the letters are colored, the whole class gets a treat or a privilege.

▲ **Book Reports.** *The Skull of Truth* is a spooky, satisfying story full of important messages about truth, integrity and friendship that could appeal to a wide range of older students. Assign the book to the class, and have them write individual book reports that address these prompts:

• Summarize the story in one paragraph.

• How did Charlie begin lying, and why did he lie?

• What happens when Charlie and those around him begin to blurt out the truth without using tact? How is tactless truth dangerous?

• While this is an intense story about serious issues, it feels light and fun to read. How does the author use humor to help the reader understand the important lessons of the story? How does he use magic and the supernatural?

• How did Yorick come to be cursed with Truth?

• After Ms. Priest told the story at the dinner table, she explained to Charlie that "...there are many kinds of truth...and that story is true in a very deep way." What do you think she meant? How can made-up stories tell the truth?

• How did Charlie patch up the damage to his friendship with Gilbert? Why was this gesture so important and effective?

• Do you think Charlie and Mark will ever be friends again? Why or why not?

Lead the class in a discussion of these questions when you collect the reports. Don't miss the opportunity to refer interested students to Shakespeare's play, *Hamlet*, to put Yorick in his original context.

Honesty Crossword

Directions: Fill in the answers to the crossword using the word bank below.

Across

2. To take something that doesn't belong to you is to _____.

5. A really big lie!

7. Everyone makes _____.

9. The voice inside that tells you what's right and wrong

11. Always tell the _____.

12. The saying goes, "_____ is the best policy."

Down

1. Never make _____ that you don't intend to keep!

3. You can _____ me to keep your secret.

4. George Washington supposedly said, "I cannot tell a _____. I chopped down the cherry tree."

6. To make something sound bigger or more important than it really was is to _____.

8. It's important to tell others the truth and to be true to _____ as well.

9. To _____ is to knowingly break the rules or give yourself an unfair advantage over others.

Word Bank

cheat	exaggerate	lie	promises	trust	whopper
conscience	honesty	mistakes	steal	truth	yourself

5 Perseverance

Perseverance is the key to getting things done and developing the habits you want. It means having a goal that matters to you and staying focused on it; working steadily and not giving up, no matter how hard it gets. People with perseverance finish what they start, and aren't afraid to make mistakes along the way. They accept challenges as they arise, and find creative ways to overcome them.

You show *perseverance* when you:

- keep trying to learn to ride your bike, even when you're tired and your knees are skinned.

- ask for help in making the model ship for your brother's birthday when it turns out to be harder than you thought.

- work at training your puppy every day, even when he or she doesn't seem to be learning.

- keep doing your long homework chapter, even though you're bored and sleepy.

- don't give up your goal to win a prize at the science fair when your first project fails.

Perseverance Resources

- *Alexander, Who is Not (Do You Hear Me? I Mean it!) Going to Move!* by Judith Viorst. Atheneum Books for Young Readers, 1995. K–2. Alexander's family is moving "a thousand miles away," and he is determined not to go. He brings oceans of perseverance to his plans to stay behind. In the end, this is one time when perseverance has to give way to the inevitable, but Alexander deserves an "A" for effort!

- *Always My Dad* by Sharon Dennis Wyeth. Alfred A. Knopf, 1995. K–3. Three young children miss their Dad, whom they rarely see. When they spend a summer with their grandparents, Dad comes to visit, and assures them of his love and his determination to "get his life together" and be there for them.

- *America's Champion Swimmer: Gertrude Ederle* by David A. Adler. Harcourt, 2000. K–5. Adler tells the story of Ederle who, in 1926, became the first woman to swim the English Channel, breaking the men's record by nearly two hours in spite of terrible weather conditions. Reporters of the day credited Ederle with shattering forever the myth of women as "the weaker sex," and President Coolidge dubbed her "America's Best Girl." A gripping and satisfying example of the power of perseverance. An ALA Notable book.

- *Apple Batter* by Deborah Turney Zagwyn. Tricycle Press, 1999. K–3. Delmore and his Mom Loretta are each crazy about two things. Each other, for one. Loretta loves gardening. Delmore loves baseball. And each has a challenge. Loretta has trouble growing apples, and Delmore can't actually hit the ball! This charming and lighthearted book tells their parallel stories of perseverance and success.

- *Apple Picking Time* by Michele Benoit Slawson. Dragonfly Books, 1994. K–2. It's apple-picking time! Anna and her family leave their usual pursuits to join the seasonal workers in the orchards. Anna wants to pick a whole bin herself. She gets tired, the apple harness digs into her shoulders, and the sun beats down. But her pride in shouting, "Full!" at the end of the day makes it all worthwhile.

- *Benjy in Business* by Jean Van Leeuwen. Dial Books for Young Readers, 1983. 2–5. Benjy really wants a new catcher's mitt he saw at the store. But he's on his own—his Mom can't buy it for him, and his birthday is months away. He sets out to earn the money. With a little help and lots of creativity and perseverance, he succeeds.

- *Captain Kate* by Carolyn Reeder. Avon Books, 1999. 4–5. Kate's family has always made their living hauling coal on the C&O Canal. It's the life Kate knows and loves, and she is devastated when her father dies and that life is threatened. Her resentment of her new stepfather, step-siblings, and even the baby her mother carries is more than she can bear. She refuses to give up on her old life, and sneaks off to take the boat down the Canal with just her stepbrother to help. The journey is full of dangers, conflicts, and self-discovery that, ultimately, lead Kate to a new maturity and acceptance of her new family.

- *Chester the Out-of-Work Dog* by Marilyn Singer. Owlet, 1997. K–3. Chester's used to herding sheep on the farm. When his family sells the farm and moves to the city, he has nothing to do. His efforts to find a new job get him and his family into all kinds of hilarious predicaments. He decides he must return to the farm, and lets nothing distract him on the way until a chance encounter gives him an opportunity to save the day and win important work.

- *Dear Dr. Bell...Your Friend, Helen Keller* by Judith St. George. Beech Tree, 1993. 4–5. St. George chronicles the friendship between Helen Keller and Alexander Graham Bell, which began when Keller was six years old. Bell was instrumental in connecting Keller with her teacher, Anne Sullivan, and remained her mentor and friend throughout his life, encouraging her to persevere in overcoming her extreme physical challenges.

- *Follow the Dream: The Story of Christopher Columbus* by Peter Sis. Random House, 1996. K–5. In lovely, richly detailed illustrations and simple, straightforward text, Sis tells of Columbus' boyhood dreams of adventure and discovery. Those dreams fueled his later determination to discover a trade route to the Orient from Europe by sailing west. To achieve his goal, he spent years learning many necessary skills, and more years being turned down by potential sponsors. But he never gave up, "and the rest is history."

- *The Glorious Flight* by Alice and Martin Provenson. Econo-Clad, 1999. K–5. On July 25, 1909, Louis Bleriot became the first person to fly across the English Channel. This Caldecott

Award Book tells how it came to be; as Bleriot spent eight years learning to fly, and then designing, building and failing with eleven models of Bleriot aircraft. A delightful look at the single-mindedness of a pioneer of aviation.

- *Hugh Can Do* by Jennifer Armstrong. Random House, 1995. K–3. Poor but optimistic Hugh must get to the city and make his fortune. Lacking the toll to cross the bridge, he takes on a humorous and creative series of swaps and deals to raise the toll. When he's almost foiled by a new toll man, the friends Hugh made along the way save the day.

- *Mistakes That Worked* by Charlotte Foltz. Doubleday, 1994. 4–5. The keynote of inventors is perseverance, and it sometimes produces surprising results! This book tells the stories of many well-known inventions that came about as "mistakes," while their inventors were pursuing other goals.

- *Misty of Chincoteague* by Marguerite Henry. Rand McNally & Co., 1947. 3–5. Paul and Maureen are staying with their grandparents on Chincoteague Island. They are in awe of the wild ponies of nearby Assateague Island, and vow to buy and tame the legendary Phantom at the next Pony Penning day. The short- and long-term results of their determined efforts are surprising and satisfying.

- *More than Anything Else* by Marie Bradby. Orchard Books, 1995. 2–4. Booker is 9, and labors with his father at the salt works. But he has a dream, a "hunger in his head," to learn to read. He longs to understand the magic and release the secrets in the mysterious black marks, and thereby become someone people listen to!

- *Mrs. Mooley* by Jack Kent. Western, 1993. K–2. Mrs. Mooley is inspired by a book of nursery rhymes left in the barn and decides that she, too, can jump over the moon—all it takes is "determination and a little practice." The

other animals laugh at her, but she perseveres. By morning, her barnyard buddies have quit laughing, and celebrate with her when she achieves her goal, after a fashion.

- *Puppet Play: The Tortoise and the Hare* by Moira Butterfield. Heinemann Library, 1998. K–5. Butterfield gives detailed instructions for making puppets and a puppet theater, and for performing the story as a puppet play.

- *Sweet Victory: Lance Armstrong's Incredible Journey* by Mark Stewart. The Millbrook Press, 2000. 3–5. Armstrong's early life, athletic career, struggle with cancer, and amazing cycling comeback are covered in this visually appealing biography. An inspiring story of pure determination.

Other Media

- *The Incredible Journey* by Walt Disney Productions, based on the novel by Sheila Every Burnford. Walt Disney Home Video, 1994 (videocassette). K–5. The heartwarming family favorite about three animals determined to make their way back to the family they love, despite all dangers and obstacles.

- "The Tortoise & the Hare" by Aesop, from *Animal Tales* as told by Jim Weiss. Greathall Productions, 1990 (CD). K–5. Weiss' highly entertaining CD includes a delightful version of the classic story about how the steady perseverance of the tortoise triumphs over the flighty vanity of the hare. Winner of multiple awards.

- *The Trumpet of the Swan* read by the author, E. B. White. Bantam, 1978 (audiobook). 3–5. Louis is a trumpeter swan born without a voice. He compensates by learning to play the trumpet! He finds joy in the music, but is determined to pay his father's debt and restore his family's honor before pursuing his personal goals, which include winning the heart of his beloved Serena.

Perseverance Activities

Discussion Prompts

Use these prompts to explore the concept of perseverance.

▲ **What's Important?** Before we can persevere, we need to know what's important to us and have a dream or a goal in mind. Lead a brainstorming session about what's important to the class, and set some goals as follows:

• What do we want to accomplish, as a class, today? What steps can we take to make sure that happens? Do we all agree to work toward that goal? How will we check, at the end of the day, to see if we accomplished our goal?

• What do we want to accomplish as a class this week? What steps can we take? Do we all agree? How can we check, at the end of the week, to see if we accomplished our goal?

Help the class set realistic goals for the day and the week. Check on progress occasionally. At the end of the day and the week, discuss the results with the class. Did you achieve your goals? What obstacles did you have to overcome? What role did perseverance play? You might follow up with one of the activities in the "Miscellaneous Activities" section on p. 47.

▲ **Personal Stories.** Share examples of story characters who had goals in mind and didn't give up, no matter what. Share a time in your life when perseverance paid off for you. Ask students to share their own stories of determination and persistence. Discuss what challenges and distractions got in the way of "sticking to it."

▲ **Realistic Goals.** In *Alexander, Who is Not (Do You Hear Me? I Mean it!) Going to Move,* Alexander has to let go of his goal because it isn't realistic. In *Captain Kate,* Kate's determination to take the boat down the canal and make money for the family without an adult puts herself and others in danger. Read or review the appropriate story with the class. Then use these ideas to stimulate discussion:

• Is perseverance toward a goal always a good thing? When might it be the best choice to give up, or at least to adjust your goal?

• Alexander and Kate were both more than determined—they were stubborn about their respective goals. Compare and contrast the ideas of "perseverance" and "stubbornness."

How can you tell if you're persevering, or just being stubborn?

Games

Use these games when students need a change of pace or a break from the work of the day.

▲ **Word Scramble.** p. 48.

▲ **The "Happy Classroom" Board Game.** Both creating and playing this game will offer exercises in perseverance—taking turns and overcoming unpredictable obstacles to get to the goal. They will also offer chances to review the character traits studied so far. To keep the game fresh, as an ongoing learning center activity, you might add cards with more examples, as well as cards for the qualities studied in later chapters. The illustration on page 46 will give you examples to work from. Follow these steps:

1) Draw a path on a piece of poster board, divided into spaces large enough for 2–4 player pieces. Sixty spaces are about right. Label the ends of the path "Start" and "Happy Classroom."

2) Provide player pieces and either dice or a numbered spinner, all of which are available at craft, game or educational supply stores. *Note: Using two dice requires students to do a little arithmetic practice with each turn.*

3) Label the board "The Happy Classroom Game," and draw on it two 3x5" rectangles. Draw or stamp a happy face on one rectangle, and a sad face on the other. Draw or stamp happy and sad faces randomly on spaces along the path, with a face on about 1/2 of the spaces. Laminate the board, to make it last longer.

4) On 3x5" index cards, create "happy" and "sad" scenarios, showing how practicing or ignoring the character traits studied so far assist or hinder in creating a happy classroom. Work with students to create the scenarios, write them on one side, and draw or stamp the appropriate face on the back. Be sure to include appropriate instructions for the player drawing the card. For example, a happy face card might read, "You invited the new kid to join your game on the playground. Move forward three spaces." A sad face card might

read, "You let your science partner down by not being prepared to demonstrate your project to the class. Skip a turn." Twenty of each kind of card should be enough to start with. Shuffle the cards and place them, face-side up, in their places on the board.

5) You're ready to play! Players take turns rolling the dice or spinning the numbered spinner and moving their player pieces accordingly. If they land on a space with a face, they draw an appropriate card and follow the instructions. The first player to arrive at the "Happy Classroom" wins the game. *Note: You might create a math tie-in by adding a word problem worksheet after the game, using questions like these: "Jeff won the game in nine turns. With 60 spaces on the board, how many spaces, on the average, did he advance per turn?"*

▲ **"Find Another Way."** In *Benjy in Business,* Benjy keeps running into problems with his business schemes, and has to think of something new to earn the money for his baseball glove. In *Hugh Can Do,* Hugh is undaunted by a complex series of creative trades aimed at getting him across the river to the city. Following those models, this simple game lets you have fun and encourage creative thinking about overcoming obstacles to achieve a goal. Pose to the class situations based on events in the stories, or of your own making, that set up a goal and an obstacle. For example, you might say, "You need information about Finland for your school report that's due tomorrow, but the library's closed. Find another way!" The class jumps in to suggest another way around the obstacle.

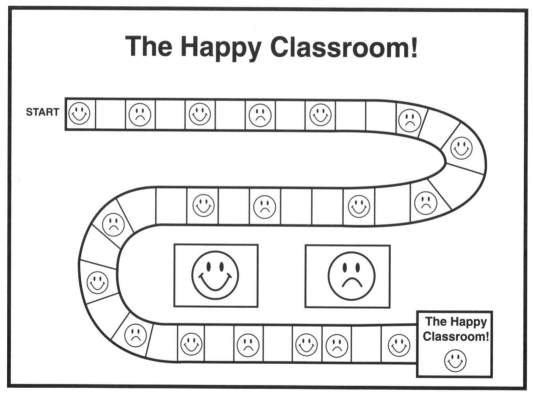

Sample "Happy Classroom" Game Board

Creative Expressions

Have fun with these creative ways to process concepts from the books on the list.

▲ **Perseverance Mottos.** Share with students some familiar sayings that relate to perseverance. Have each student either choose one of the sayings you provide, or make up a new perseverance motto of his or her own, and create an illustrated poster or display for the class that expresses and explains the saying. Some examples:

• "Slow and steady wins the race."

• "Hang in there!"

• "Don't give up the ship!"

• "The snail reached the ark by perseverance."

• "Rome wasn't built in a day."

• "One step at a time."

▲ **"The Tortoise and the Hare" Puppet Play.** Start by sharing with students a good version of the Aesop fable. You might use the CD version listed in the bibliography. Then use the book *Puppet Play: The Tortoise and the Hare* to create the characters and set, and rehearse and present the play for another class.

▲ **Creating with Clay.** Clay is a medium that requires perseverance, just by its nature! Have each student choose a favorite book from the chapter bibliography, and create a clay sculpture that expresses something from the book. Students can show and tell about their sculptures for the rest of the class.

▲ **Perseverance Journal.** Have students decorate the front of a journal or notebook. At the beginning of each day during this unit, give them a few minutes to review earlier goals and to set personal goals for the day. At the end of each day, give them time to reflect on and write about their progress toward their goals, and any victories or obstacles encountered. If you had students begin journals for the Responsibility chapter, they could continue in the same book.

▲ **"What's Important to You?"** *Follow the Dream: The Story of Christopher Columbus*, and *More than Anything Else* both tell of deeply cherished, important dreams held in childhood that inspired genuine perseverance. While not every elementary student has a driving life's dream or goal in mind, some do! As an extra credit assignment, invite students to write or record on audiocassette an essay about a dream or life ambition—something they long to do or to become—that's very important to them. You might be surprised at the hidden talents or lofty aspirations you discover and find ways to nurture them.

Miscellaneous Activities

Try these activities to help students understand the concepts and practice of perseverance.

▲ **Accomplished Members of the Community.** Invite one or more guests to visit the class, who have accomplished important things in the community. You might choose someone who lead the way toward solving a community problem or meeting a social need, or someone who has created a successful business, or perhaps one of each. Have your guests talk about the role of perseverance in their successes. Prepare the students in advance to ask good questions about the process of choosing and pursuing their goals, the challenges that had to be overcome along the way and the creative solutions that were found to address them.

▲ **Class Service Project.** Consult about a project to take on together that would be meaningful and important to the members of the class. Perhaps it could be another service project, as suggested in the Caring chapter. Or it might be inspired by the achievements of one of the guests invited for the preceding activity. For example, if you invited a guest who started a weekend class to teach families about safety, you might decide as a class to develop a safety newsletter for the school. Make a plan and persevere to successfully complete the project.

▲ **Recipes.** Read *Apple Batter* and *Apple Picking Time* with the class. Talk about the goals and ambitions of the characters, and how they persevered to achieve them. Then choose one of the recipes (there's one in each book) and let the class bake an apple treat together.

▲ **Succeeding Against the Odds.** In *Dear Mr. Bell…Your Friend, Helen Keller* and in *Sweet Victory: Lance Armstrong's Incredible Journey*, we learn about people who overcame enormous physical challenges to accomplish great things in their lives. Assign students to individually identify and research other people with physical or mental illnesses or disabilities who persevered and succeeded against the odds.

Perseverance Word Scramble

Directions: Unscramble the following words related to perseverance by drawing lines between the scrambled word and its unscrambled match.

ufocs	mistakes
nidrenemtiato	habits
olgsa	determination
hiinfs	steady
caveprseerne	focus
tydsae	perseverance
eaitksms	obstacles
elsbatosc	creative
victraee	goals
thisab	finish

6 Courage

When we think of *courage*, we often picture bravery in battle or a daring rescue. That's part of the story. But there's more to courage than dramatic feats of physical strength. Courage is really about standing up for yourself and others, even when it's uncomfortable or dangerous. It means doing what's right in the face of difficulty, and listening to your conscience, rather than to the crowd. Courageous people aren't fearless; they just don't let fear control them. They try new things that make them nervous, so they can grow. And they don't take foolish risks or boast to impress others—real courage is facing your fears and doing what's right, no matter what.

You show *courage* when you:

- defend a smaller child from a bully.

- stand up for a classmate who is being teased because he or she is different.

- refuse a dare to do something wrong or dangerous.

- agree to speak in front of the whole school at an assembly.

- tell an adult, *"No!"* when he or she tries to touch you inappropriately.

- agree to try a new game in front of everyone, even when you think you might not be good at it.

- comfort your little brother or sister during a thunderstorm, even though you're afraid, too.

■ *Arnie and the Skateboard Gang* by Nancy Carlson. Viking Press, 1995. K–2. Arnie and Tina get good enough on their skateboards to join the cool gang at the park. But when the gang decides to try out a dangerous hill, Arnie has to decide how much he'll risk to be cool. A good "stand up for yourself" story.

■ *Captain Snap and the Children of Vinegar Lane* by Roni Schotter. Orchard Books, 1993. K–3. The children of Vinegar Lane have a favorite pastime. They sneak down and shout at the scary, crazy old man at the end of the lane, who never talks and keeps to himself. Then they run away, thrilled with their audacity. But when they find Captain Snap ill, they feel obliged to help, no matter how scared they are. And in doing the right thing, they discover a world of wonders and a new friend.

■ *Colin Powell: Straight to the Top* by Rose Blue and Corinne J. Naden. Milbrook Press, 1997. 3–5. This appealing biography tells about Powell's life and illustrious military and civilian careers, stressing his perseverance, courage, and quiet competence. Whether tackling racism, battling an enemy on foreign soil, or negotiating diplomatic solutions to national or international problems, Powell has proved himself a hero of contemporary American life.

■ *Courage, Dana* by Susan Beth Pfeffer. Delacorte Press, 1983. 2–5. Dana is timid by nature. But when she sees a little boy run out into traffic, she acts without thinking and saves his life. The experience and resulting celebrity go to Dana's head. But, ultimately, they cause Dana, and the people around her, to think of her in a new way, to revise their notions about courage, and to stand up to the school bully together.

■ *Girls to the Rescue, Book #6* edited by Bruce Lansky. Meadowbrook Press, 1999. 2–4. This series of "tales of clever, courageous girls from around the world" brings together nine stories by different authors. These particular stories feature a niece of the fictional Sherlock Holmes, a Chinese girl who stands up for her right to an education, and a young African American slave who leads her younger brother to freedom via the Underground Railway.

■ *Harriet and the Promised Land* by Jacob Lawrence. Simon & Schuster, 1993. K–5. With bold, engaging art and tight, rhythmic text, this book shares highlights from life of Harriet Tubman. Born into slavery, she not only freed herself, but also served as a "conductor" on the Underground Railroad, leading over 300 slaves to freedom in the north, and went on to fight for women's suffrage and to support the Union in the Civil War. The drama of Tubman's life is effectively reflected in Lawrence's book, which could serve as an introduction to a deeper study of this genuine American heroine.

■ *Kate Shelley: Bound for Legend* by Robert D. San Souci. Dial Books for Young Readers, 1995. 2–5. Fifteen-year-old Kate Shelley, an ordinary Iowa farm girl, risked her life in a terrible rainstorm to save the survivors of a train wreck near her home, and to warn an oncoming train of danger ahead. Her great courage and selflessness, described in this biography, made her famous across the nation.

■ *A Little Excitement* by Ted Rand. Penguin Putnam, 1994. K–3. When Willie wishes for excitement during a long winter, he gets more than he bargained for. The family wakes up in the night to a fire in the chimney, and must overcome their fear and work together to save their home.

■ *Little Polar Bear and the Brave Little Hare* by Hans DeBeer. North-South Books, 1992. 1–2. In this beginning reader, a polar bear saves a frightened little hare during a winter storm. The two get lost, and Hugo the Hare whimpers with fear about everything around him. But when the bear is in danger, Hugo finds the courage to save him in return.

■ *One of the Third Grade Thonkers* by Phyllis Reynolds Naylor. Econo-Clad, 1999. 3–5. The Thonkers are the toughest, bravest third-graders of all. Jimmy, their leader, is riding high on the glory of surviving knee surgery. He worries about his image when his babyish cousin David comes to stay. But then Jimmy's family faces a crisis. Jimmy learns about real courage and is forced to credit David with having it where it counts. A Children's Choice book.

■ *Papa!* by Philippe Corentin. Chronicle Books, 1997. K–2. What parent hasn't been called to rescue children from monsters in bed at night? This clever picture book turns the tables on our expectations, and shares the loving parental comfort aimed at both sides of the bed! A delightful look at fear of the dark and the unknown.

- *The Paper Dragon* by Marguerite W. Davol. Atheneum Books for Young Readers, 1997. K–5. Mi Fei is a humble artist, content, despite his growing fame, to paint the old stories and the people of the village he loves. But his peaceful life is disrupted when a great dragon awakes and begins laying waste the countryside. The villagers beg Mi Fei to face the dragon, and though he is frightened, he can't refuse. With quiet courage and cleverness, Mi Fei arises in spite of his fear, and releases both the people and the dragon from their ordeals.

- *Seven Brave Women* by Betsy Hearne. Greenwillow Books, 1997. K–5. Hearne tells of seven women over five generations in her family who faced lives full of challenge with day-to-day courage. Their quiet strength is contrasted with the more commonly recognized bravery of men in war during their lifetimes.

- *The Tale of Custard the Dragon* by Ogden Nash. Little, Brown & Co., 1998. K–3. Custard the "realio, trulio little pet dragon," is certain that everyone in his house is braver than he, and wants nothing more than his nice, safe cage, until a pirate arrives to threaten his little family. While Belinda, the dog, the kitten and the mouse all make excuses and seek to escape, Custard rises to the occasion. A delightful story in rhyme about courage as deeds, not words.

- *Thunder Cake* by Patricia Polacco. Philomel Books, 1990. K–3. A child's babushka (grandma) helps her to face her fear of the oncoming storm by baking Thunder Cake.

- **"What Was I Scared Of?"** by Dr. Seuss. From *The Sneetches and Other Stories*. Random House, 1997. K–3. Our hero has much to say about his bravery, until he is confronted with a spooky pair of pants "with nobody inside them." In fine Seuss style, he describes his waning courage and growing fear. Then, to his surprise, he discovers that the pants are scared of him, too! An entertaining lesson about fear of the unknown, and its remedy.

- *Wringer* by Jerry Spinelli. HarperTrophy Books, 1997. 4–5. This Newbery Honor Book is a disturbing story of a young boy caught between his feelings and the cruel expectations of a long-standing community tradition. Each year his town concludes its big family celebration with a contest to see who can shoot the most pigeons. Ten-year-old boys serve as "wringers," wringing the necks of the birds that are wounded rather than killed. Palmer doesn't want to be a wringer, but also dreads being labeled a coward and ostracized by his peers. His dilemma is magnified when a stray pigeon befriends him. Not for all students, but mature readers will find much to think about as Palmer struggles with fears, feelings, beliefs and courage.

Other Media

- *The Courage of Sarah Noble* by Alice Dalgliesh. Recorded Books, Inc., 1998 (audiobook). K–3. The classic story of real-life Sarah Noble is told in this unabridged audiobook version. Sarah traveled with her father to the wilderness to cook for him while he built a home for their family, and had to constantly replay her mother's words to "Keep up your courage, Sarah Noble." The greatest challenge came when Sarah had to stay behind with their Indian neighbors while her father went to bring the rest of the family.

- *Sheila Rae, the Brave* by Kevin Henkes. Living Books, 1996 (interactive CD-ROM). K–2. Sheila Rae is fearless and proud of it! She shows off her bravery, and calls her sister a scaredy-cat. But when she decides to try a new way home and gets lost, her famous courage dissolves in tears, and guess who saves the day! A lighthearted look at what courage is and is not.

Courage Activities

Discussion Prompts

Use these prompts to explore the concept of courage.

▲ **"What Makes a Hero?"** Lead a discussion on the meaning heroism, using these questions:

• Who do you think of when you hear the word "hero?"

• What makes those people heroes? What actions or qualities are heroic?

• Are heroes always famous people? Do they always become famous? Do they always do big, dramatic things, like Superman saving the world from destruction?

• Some people are heroes because they do daring things to protect or rescue others. Give examples. (Students might think of fire fighters, emergency medical crews, police officers, etc.)

• Some people are heroes because they have strong beliefs and are willing to stand up for themselves and their beliefs even when others are cruel or violent toward them. Can you think of examples? (Mention victims of religious persecution, pacifists, or Civil Rights workers.)

• Now that we've talked about different kinds of heroes, can you think of others?

▲ **Real Courage.** Talk with students about events in the stories where characters showed real courage. Share a time in your experience when you faced a personal fear or did something courageous. Invite students to share anecdotes from their own lives when they were able to show courage. Use the discussion to round out students' understanding of what courage really means.

▲ **"What Was I Scared Of?"** To start this discussion, read Dr. Seuss' *What Was I Scared Of?*. Explain that everyone is afraid of something. (One of the things that frightens Dana in *Courage, Dana* is that she'll never do anything brave again. Sometimes we're afraid of looking cowardly!) Use these questions to stimulate discussion of the things that people fear.

• What things were characters from the books in the bibliography afraid of? (Sarah Noble feared strange sounds in the dark and staying with the Indians, the children of Vinegar Lane feared their unusual neighbor, the child in *Thunder Cake* feared the oncoming storm, etc.)

• What are some other things that people are afraid of?

• While the fear people feel is always a real feeling, not all of the things they're afraid of are real dangers. For example, thunder is just sound, darkness is just the absence of light and monsters aren't real. Can you think of other examples of things people are afraid of that aren't real dangers?

• What could you do to face your fear of something real (like the fire in *A Little Excitement*)? You might talk about learning safety tips and having family fire drills so you're prepared.

• What could you do to face your fear of something that doesn't represent a real danger (like the thunder in *Thunder Cake*)? You might discuss learning all you can about the object of your fear, and finding ways to distract yourself or make a game of facing the fear.

▲ **Outside Your Comfort Zone.** Sometimes it takes real courage to express your honest feelings, or to try something new that's worthwhile but makes you feel nervous or uncomfortable. Give examples, like singing a solo, telling a friend you're disappointed in his behavior or reading a poem you wrote aloud to the class. Ask the class for other examples. Next, have the class spend a moment quietly (students should not be pressed to reveal their personal fears) thinking about things that frighten them, personally. Then have them think, still silently, about something worthwhile they could try to learn or do that would take courage—something that would involve taking a risk, feeling a bit nervous or uncomfortable or standing out. Stress that these things must be safe, and must be things their parents would approve of. Encourage students to act on their ideas. Offer to help students who could use your assistance to take a risk and try something new.

Note: Papier Mâché Monsters *in Creative Expressions would be a good follow-up to the* Real Courage *and* "What Was I Scared Of?" *Discussion Prompts above.*

Games

Use these games when students need a change of pace or a break from the work of the day.

▲ **Synonyms and Antonyms.** As individuals or as a class have students brainstorm as many synonyms as they can for "courage" or "courageous." Then do the same for antonyms. You might supplement the vocabulary value of this game by adding words like "intrepid," "dauntlessness," "fortitude," "timidity" or "faintheartedness."

▲ **Courage Anagram.** Follow up the previous exercise using the reproducible handout on p. 55, which invites students to find anagrams based on the word, "Courageous." There are at least 265 such words, so students should have lots to find, and might enjoy comparing their results.

▲ **"Catch & Tell."** This game, introduced in Chapter 1, could be used to help students recognize quiet, everyday acts of courage in one another. Challenge students to "catch" each other being brave, and to tell the teacher about it! Add the name of each student caught showing courage to a list on the board headed, "Catch & Tell: These students were caught being courageous this week."

Creative Expressions

Have fun with these creative ways to process concepts from the books on the list.

▲ **Papier Mâché Monsters.** Read with the class *Papa!* and/or *The Paper Dragon.* In both stories, the characters are afraid of a beast or monster. Imaginary beasts or monsters are often symbols for danger or for the things we fear. Invite students to think about the things that frighten them, and then to create a monster from papier mâché that represents the objects of their fears. Provide a variety of materials, including plastic jars or bottles, cardboard tubes, or different sized and shaped balloons to form the basic shape of the monsters. Then cover the shapes with papier mâché. A very simple way to do papier mâché is to have students dip 1" strips of newspaper in white glue until they are coated, and apply them to the basic shapes to add bulk and texture. Once the forms are dried, they can be painted with acrylic or poster paint and completed using pipe cleaners,

buttons, plastic eyes and other craft materials. You could enhance the symbolism for older students by having them write their private fears on small slips of paper, and insert them into the balloons or cardboard bases for their monsters. When the monsters are complete, invite students who are willing to share why they made their monsters the way they did. Then vote as a class for the scariest monster!

▲ **Story-poems.** Read *Custard the Dragon* aloud to the class. Have students try their hands at writing and illustrating, or recording on audiocassette, their own light-hearted story-poems about acts of bravery.

▲ **Heroes.** This two-part activity combines research opportunities with a variety of creative expressions.

Part One: First, have each student choose a figure from history that he or she sees as a real hero. You might introduce this part of the activity by reading or reviewing *Kate Shelley: Bound for Legend.* Have students learn as much as they can about their heroes. Then students are to find creative ways to share part of their heroes' stories with the class. They might dress up like the person and talk to the class as though the hero was speaking. Or they might read short stories, essays or poems they found or wrote about their heroes.

Part Two: Each student will choose a contemporary hero—someone living today. You might introduce this part by reviewing *Colin Powell: Straight to the Top.* It might help to offer a starting list of individuals appropriate to your community and the age of your students. Encourage students to consider "everyday heroes," as well as famous people. Next, students are to learn all they can about their living hero. Urge students to interview their heroes in person, or to write them letters, if possible. Again, students will find creative ways to share their heroes' stories with the class. Students might report on an interview, read their letters and the responses from their heroes, or create posters showing highlights from their heroes' lives. This activity would tie in nicely with activities in the "Miscellaneous Activities" section below.

Note: Resources for researching heroes might include these web sites. **The Academy of Achievement Museum at www.achievement.org** *leads you through a virtual museum, featuring "extraordinary individuals who have shaped the twentieth century." The Hall of Courage offers quotations, audio and video information on a variety of historic and contemporary heroes.* **"Giraffe Country" at www.giraffe.org** *welcomes you to a program that* *seeks to recognize people from everyday life who "stick their necks out" for the common good. Go to "looking for stories about heroes" for reports of "giraffe sitings" of contemporary heroes, young and old.*

Miscellaneous Activities

Try these activities to help students understand the concepts and practice of courage.

▲ **Courage Journal.** Continuing the journal developed for the Responsibility and Perseverance chapters, have students take time to reflect on and record their personal fears, and come up with ideas for facing and overcoming them. Then invite them to write about a goal to try something new that is worthwhile and feels like a risk. Reassure students that their journals are private; they are not expected to share their personal fears with anyone else. It would be wise to provide a safe place to store the journals that will guarantee confidentiality.

▲ **The Courage of Escaped Slaves.** Review *Harriet and the Promised Land.* Invite interested students to research the Underground Railroad, organized to smuggle slaves to freedom in the North. Discuss the heroic risks taken by those who hid runaway slaves, because of their beliefs, as well as the courage of the slaves who risked their lives to flee slavery.

▲ **Recognizing Heroes.** Consider one or more of these ways to recognize acts of courage and heroism.

• Develop a class award for courage in action, to recognize someone living in the community who has shown exceptional courage. The class might want to name the award after a favorite historical, contemporary or local hero. Have the class review their understanding of courage, and decide who might qualify for the award. Then have students nominate and vote for a winner. Design a medal as a prize for the winner.

• Plan an award ceremony to honor the winner. Invite the winner, along with parents and any of the students' contemporary heroes, from the Creative Expressions activity above, who might attend. Plan an appropriate program to introduce and credit the award-winner, and to introduce other special guests. You might consider presenting this program and refreshments as a special assembly for the whole school.

• Visit the www.giraffe.org web site mentioned above. Read about The Giraffe Heroes Program, and download the nomination form. Consult together about the nomination criteria of risk ("sticking your neck out") and common good. Nominate someone from your community to be the program's newest "Giraffe."

▲ **Book Discussion Groups.** Assign older readers to three groups. One group will read *One of the Third Grade Thonkers*, another *Courage, Dana*, and the third *Wringer* (See the caution in the bibliography about this title). After reading the books, each group should discuss what their book had to say about courage, using these questions:

• How did individuals show courage in this book? Did the characters show physical courage, or the courage of their convictions, or both? Were there examples of cowardly behavior in this book?

• What role did peer pressure play in the book? How did the expectations or the reactions of other kids affect the main character's actions?

• What did you learn about courage that might help you in your own life?

Each group should select a spokesperson to give a short book review and summary of the group's discussion to the other groups.

Courage Anagram

Directions: Anagrams are a group of letters found in another word, used as the source word. See how many words you can find using the letters in the source word below. There's a sample to get you started.

COURAGEOUS

rags

_____   _____   _____

_____   _____   _____

_____   _____   _____

_____   _____   _____

_____   _____   _____

_____   _____   _____

_____   _____   _____

_____   _____   _____

_____   _____   _____

_____   _____   _____

_____   _____   _____

_____   _____   _____

7 Self-discipline

Just as courage is not being controlled by your fears, *self-discipline* is not being controlled by every impulsive thought or feeling that comes over you. Self-discipline means will power—taking charge of yourself and choosing how to act, based on a set of internal rules. We all feel lazy, rebellious, greedy, selfish, frustrated or angry sometimes. If we always act on those feelings, other people have to control us so we don't hurt each other or ourselves. But if we are self-disciplined, we control our own behavior and are more independent and organized. Self-disciplined people create and follow routines, habits and rules for themselves that bring order to their lives, help them get along well with others, and accomplish their goals.

You show *self-discipline* when you:

- stop and count to 10 (or 100!) before confronting someone you're mad at.

- decide not to buy the candy you want right now, because you'd rather save your money for a new skateboard.

- do your homework first, so you'll be able to watch your favorite TV show later.

- force yourself to practice for basketball tryouts, even though you'd rather take a nap.

- choose not to eat the last cupcake, because you know they're your sister's favorite, and she's had a bad day.

- choose to explain your strong feelings, rather than using meaningless cuss words.

Self-discipline Resources

- *Andrew's Angry Words* by Dorothea Lachner. North-South Books, 1995. K-3. When things go wrong for Andrew, he hurls a bunch of angry words, starting a chain reaction of anger that extends from land to air to sea, and from motorcycle riders to dragons and princesses. The angry words are finally replaced with kind words, causing a reverse chain reaction. A good example of how unbridled anger breeds more anger and harm.

- *The Ant and the Grasshopper* by Amy Lowry Poole. Holiday House, 2000. K-5. This lovely retelling of the classic Aesop fable is set in the Imperial gardens of the Qing Dynasty. As a bonus to the story about the consequences of self-indulgence and self-discipline, the author-illustrator includes a note about the palaces and gardens that inspired her setting, and the media and processes used to illustrate the book, offering tie-ins to history and art.

- *Ape Ears and Beaky* by Nancy J. Hopper. E. P. Dutton, 1984. 3-5. Scott has a problem with his temper—bad enough that he's seeing a counselor. But a strange turn of events teams him up with one of the people who irritate him, to catch a couple of thieves. As the various subplots unfold, he learns to take charge of himself and do what's right.

- *The Boy of the Three-Year Nap* by Dianne Snyder. Troll, 1999. K-3. When lazy Taro connives to marry the rich neighbor's daughter, his mother carries the plan a step farther. In addition to gaining a rich lifestyle for the family, Taro finds himself gaining a challenging job as well. In the end, everyone lives happily ever after. A Caldecott Honor Book.

- *Elbert's Bad Word* by Audrey Wood. Harcourt Brace, 1996. K-3. A bad word slips into Elbert's mouth, and then jumps out at a crucial moment, shocking everyone at the garden party. Elbert earns a mouth washing. But he knows where to go for help, and the next time he has an angry impulse, more creative and appropriate words replace the curse. Don't we all wish we had a wizard to rescue us when we give in to our impulses?

- *Francine, Believe It or Not* by Stephen Krensky. Little, Brown and Co., 1999. 1-3. In this Marc Brown Arthur Chapter Book Series title, Francine takes a bet that she can't keep her temper and be nice for a whole week. It's really hard, but she comes through.

- *From the Mixed-up Files of Mrs. Basil E. Frankweiler* by E. L. Konigsburg. Scholastic, 1997. 3-5. Claudia and James decide to run away, as a combination of adventure and protest against perceived unfairness at home. They plan carefully, and show great creativity and self-control as they hide out in the New York Metropolitan Museum of Art, where they get caught up in a mystery. A Newbery Award Book.

- *Harriet, You'll Drive Me Wild!* By Mem Fox. Harcourt, Inc., 2000. K–3. Harriet doesn't mean to be difficult, and she's always sorry after. Her careless behavior tests her mother's self-control as well. This sweet story shows both Harriet and her mother trying to cope.

- *Inside of Me There's a Storm a-Brewing* by Nancy Lee Walker. Naturally by Nan Publishing, 1996. K–3. This spiral bound picture book effectively uses black and white photos of mimes and foldout inserts to illustrate a simple narrative about the choices we have when intense emotions threaten to take us over. The last few pages set up a simple game that continues exploring choices.

- *Jamie O'Rourke and the Pooka* by Tomie dePaola. G. P. Putnam's Sons, 2000. K–3. When lazy Jamie's wife leaves for a week, he promises to keep things in shape. But his buddies visit and they eat, drink and carry on, leaving Jamie too tired to clean. He's surprised by an enchanted pooka, who comes in the night and cleans up the messes. In a clever twist, the pooka cons Jamie into releasing him from his pooka curse, earned by his own laziness during his lifetime, leaving Jamie to "face the music" with his wife. An endnote explains the origin of the pooka legend.

- *Mean Soup* by Betsy Everitt. Harcourt Brace Jovanovich, 1992. K–2. Horace has had a bad day, and he's mad. But his clever, understanding mother helps him work off his anger in a creative (rather than hurtful) way.

- *Rip-Roaring Russell* by Johanna Hurwitz. Harper Collins, 2001. 1–2. Russell has a tendency to lose his temper, and to give in to his impulses. We see him go through good times and bad, as his parents and teacher work with him and help him learn some small life lessons.

- *Rumpelstiltskin's Daughter* by Diane Stanley. Morrow Junior Books, 1997. K–5. In this revision and sequel to the original tale, Rumpelstiltskin's daughter is locked up by the king to spin straw to gold. But the clever girl uses the king's greed to fuel a plan designed to both fool and educate the king, while aiding his starving subjects. The story illustrates how those without self-control are vulnerable to the control of others, for better or worse.

- *Tough Loser* by Barthe DeClements. Viking Press, 1994. 3–5. Siblings Mike and Jenna both have problems with self-discipline. Jenna's a yeller, and Mike can't control his anger when his hockey team loses. When they both have something at stake that really matters to them, they help and encourage each other to stop and think before they act.

- *Understood Betsy* by Dorothy Canfield Fisher. Henry Holt, 1999. 3–5. Spoiled, overprotected Elizabeth Ann is terrified when she must go to live with "those awful Putney cousins." To her horror, they expect her to help out, know how to do things for herself, and have her own ideas! But she finds that she enjoys it, and takes pride in this new girl, "Betsy," that she is becoming. The satisfying story suggests that self-reliance and self-discipline must be modeled and taught, and that the results are happiness and strength of character.

- *Wilma Unlimited: How Wilma Rudolph Became the World's Fastest Woman* by Kathleen Krull. Harcourt Brace & Company, 1996. 2–5. Wilma Rudolph was born very small and suffered polio as a child. She was barely expected to live, let alone walk. But from a young age, Wilma pushed herself to conquer her physical challenges. Aided by her family's support, Wilma refused to give in to pain, teasing, sadness and exhaustion, and went on to become a triple-winner in the 1960 Summer Olympics. An astounding story of will power and self-discipline.

Other Media

- *How the Rhinoceros Got His Skin* by Rudyard Kipling. Rabbit Ears Productions, 1989 (book and audiobook). K–5. This delightful version, narrated by Jack Nicholson, with music by Bobby McFerrin, tells of the terrible mistake the rhinoceros makes by stealing the Parsee man's cake. As punishment for his greed, he is cursed to live forever with wrinkled, itchy skin full of cake crumbs that tickle and irritate.

- *Winnie the Pooh and the Honey Tree* based on the story by A. A. Milne. Walt Disney Animated Storybook (Interactive CD-ROM). K–2. In this familiar and beloved story, Winnie the Pooh is a victim of his own greed for honey, causing problems for himself and his friends. The interactive format allows for side trips into music or other activities.

- *Beethoven Violin Concerto, Bernstein Serenade* performed by Hilary Hahn. Sony, 1999 (CD). K–5. Youthful prodigy Hilary Hahn was in her teens when she made this recording, but started studying violin at age four, and debuted with the Baltimore Symphony Orchestra at age nine. She did her schoolwork at home, and practiced her instrument for 5 1/2 hours a day. You might use this as background, or for quiet listening in the classroom, drawing attention to the discipline required for a young musician to make it in the competitive world of classical music.

Self-discipline Activities

Discussion Prompts

Use these prompts to explore the concept of self-discipline.

▲ **Self-discipline in Daily Life.** Lead a discussion appropriate to the age of your students about what things in their lives require self-discipline. Use examples from the stories. For example, in *Francine, Believe it or Not*, Francine needs to control what she chooses to say to her friends, and how she says it; as well as how she plays with her team in street hockey. Brainstorm with students, writing ideas on the board.

• When might you need to use self-control at school? At home? On the playground? In sports or games? In music, dance or other lessons?

• What goal can you set to have more self-discipline with your schoolwork? At home? With friends or classmates?

Goals can be recorded in student journals, to make it easier for you to encourage students to review their goals and monitor their progress.

▲ **Needs vs. Wants.** Sometimes we get into trouble because we don't understand the difference between needs and wants. Part of self-discipline is making sure we have enough of what we need, but not feeling entitled to more of what we want than is good for us. In *Rip-Roaring Russell*, Russell throws tantrums when he doesn't get to go to a parade or can't stay home from school and act like his baby sister. And in *From the Mixed-up Files of Mr. Basil E. Frankweiler*, Claudia, who has plenty of self-discipline in some areas, decides to run away from home because she doesn't feel adequately appreciated. Explore needs and wants using these questions:

• What things do we really *need* to stay alive and healthy physically and emotionally and to grow and contribute to our families and communities? (List those things on the board. They should include basics like nutritious food, clothes, shelter, love, education, medical care, etc.)

• If those are our real needs, then what is everything else? (Wants!)

• What are some things we *want*, in addition to what we *need*? (List some of those things, too.)

Point out that it's good to have some of what we want. But expecting to get everything we want is excessive and not good for us. Self-discipline helps us to accept sensible limits, and to limit ourselves in sensible ways.

▲ **Flexing Our Self-discipline Muscles.** Self-discipline is a little like a muscle. If we want to develop it, get better at it and keep it in shape, we have to make a point of using it. To be sure we have enough self-control and will power when we really need it, it helps to "exercise the muscle" often. These can be serious exercises, like refusing to spread gossip. Or they can be fun, silly exercises, like putting one of your favorite cookies in front of you while you study or watch TV, and seeing how long you can hold off before you eat it! Have students suggest simple "exercises" they might do to keep their self-discipline "muscles" strong.

▲ **Dealing with Anger.** Anger is a difficult and dangerous issue for many people who lack self-control. Read *Mean Soup*, and talk about how Horace's mother helped him get out his frustrations safely and creatively. Brainstorm other safe, creative ways students might vent their anger, and make a list as a resource to send home with students. Some examples might be to punch your pillow, have a good cry by yourself, run around the block a few times, draw an angry picture or write an angry letter and then throw it away. Point out that shouting the first bad word that comes to mind is not only lazy, it's meaningless—it doesn't give any information about what's bothering you. Sometimes things that anger us are best left alone. But when they need to be talked about, it's important to choose meaningful ways to express our thoughts and feelings that allow others to understand and work with us at making things better.

Games

Use these games when students need a change of pace or a break from the work of the day.

▲ **Mystery Word Game.** p. 62. The answer to this puzzle is "willpower."

▲ **"Grandma's Rule" Game.** You might introduce this game by reading *The Ant and the Grasshopper*. The game helps students understand the difference between things we have to do and things we want to do, and how those concepts relate to self-discipline. Explain the simple guideline, commonly known as "Grandma's Rule," that "have to's" should be done before "want to's." Then follow these steps.

1) Have students write on small slips of paper two things they like to do, and two things they have to do. Give examples, like playing ball for the former and washing dishes for the latter.

2) Collect the slips of paper. Put the "have to's" in one box and the "want to's" in another. Keep the boxes in a bigger box that students can't see into, so you can change the positions of the smaller boxes between turns.

3) Call students up to draw a slip of paper from each smaller box.

4) Have students decide, on the basis of "Grandma's Rule," which to do first.

▲ **"Stoplight," or the Choice Game.** Begin by reading *Inside Me There's a Storm a-Brewing*. The last few pages suggest, first with pictures and words, and then with just pictures, several scenarios that have to do with choosing how to act on strong feelings. Use the book to elicit possible choices from students, and then help students develop their own scenarios of things that might cause strong feelings. In the "Stoplight" variation, follow these steps:

1) Draw a large stoplight on poster board. Write "Feel," "Think," and "Act" on the red, yellow and green circles, respectively. (See illustration below.)

2) Have students come up with situations that might make them feel angry, greedy, lazy, or self-indulgent in other ways. You may need to give examples from the books, or offer your own suggestions to get things started.

3) As you identify each situation, cover the yellow and green lights to show "Feel." Point out that when you have a strong, impulsive response to a situation, it's wise to take a minute to think before acting.

4) Next, cover red and green to show "Think." Brainstorm as a class, or call on an individual student, to suggest ways you might react to the situation. Don't judge reactions at this point, just get ideas out.

5) Finally, cover red and yellow to show "Act." Let students choose the best response to the situation, and talk about probable consequences as appropriate.

Use this game to reinforce the idea that we can't always control the things that happen to us, but we can always choose how we will act in response. Taking time to think and choose carefully can help keep us and others safe and out of trouble!

Creative Expressions

Have fun with these creative ways to process concepts from the books on the list.

▲ **Strong Words for Strong Feelings.** Read *Elbert's Bad Word* and/or *Andrew's Angry Words*. Talk about the need for strong words to express strong feelings, and the equally important need to show respect and courtesy by using appropriate words and not hurting people's feelings unnecessarily. While we might all wish for a wizard to help us fix our problems, most often we have to figure them out for ourselves! Have students create lists of strong words that will help them express and explain strong feelings appropriately and not get them in trouble. Refer back to *Elbert* for examples to get them started. Then have each student choose his or her favorite strong word to add to a class collage, which can be illustrated and posted in the classroom, to remind students to choose appropriate, inoffensive ways to express their feelings.

▲ **Lack of Self-discipline.** Read or review the stories that relate to anger (*Elbert's Bad Word* or *Andrew's Angry Words*), greed (*Rumpelstiltskin's Daughter, How the Rhinoceros got his Skin* or *Winnie the Pooh and the Honey Tree*) and laziness (*Jamie O'Rourke and the Pooka* or *The Boy of the Three-Year Nap*). Then divide the class into small groups to create original fables or tales about what happens to a character who lacks self-discipline in one of these ways. Each group should read or act out their story for the class.

▲ **Song Lyrics.** Invite students to choose a well-known song and rewrite the lyrics to tell a story about using self-discipline. Encourage students to perform their songs for the class.

Miscellaneous Activities

Try these activities to help students understand the concepts and practice of self-discipline.

▲ **Self-discipline Journal.** Continuing in the journal developed for earlier chapters, have students take time to reflect on and record their personal strengths and challenges in the area of self-control and come up with goals for improving. You might encourage older students to begin to explore their own set of "internal rules" by which they control, or want to control, their own behavior. What are the rules they try not to break in dealing with themselves and others? What qualities and values are important to them? What kind of behavior makes them feel best about themselves? Reassure students that their journals are private; they are not expected to share their personal challenges, values or goals with anyone else. Provide a safe place to store the journals that will guarantee confidentiality.

▲ **Success and Self-discipline.** Review *Wilma Unlimited.* Talk together about people in the community, possibly business professionals, artists or athletes, who have achieved success in their fields. Invite one or more of these people to speak to the class about the role of self-discipline in their success. Prepare students to treat these guests with respect and courtesy, and to ask good questions that explore the role of any of the qualities discussed in this book in their efforts and successes.

▲ **Book Discussion Groups.** Assign older readers to three groups. One group will read *Tough Loser,* another *From the Mixed-up Files of Mrs. Basil E. Frankweiler,* and the third *Ape Ears and Beaky.* After reading the books, each group should discuss what role self-discipline, or lack of it, played in their book, using these questions:

• What characters showed self-discipline in the book? Which characters lacked self-discipline? Were there any characters who were very self-controlled in some ways but not in others?

• Each book showed main characters in important relationships with peers or family members. How did the relationships in the books help the main characters solve their problems and grow? Were there adults in the book that helped the young characters solve their problems and learn something important? How did they help?

• What did you learn about self-discipline that might help you in your own life?

Each group should select a spokesperson to give a short book review and summary of the group's discussion to the other groups.

▲ **Child Prodigies.** Invite students to listen to the Hilary Hahn CD, and then research other child prodigies in the visual or performing arts. Students should report back to the class in a format that showcases the talents and accomplishments of the artist.

Mystery Word Game

Directions: Solve the puzzle by filling in the missing words from the word bank below. Then unscramble the circled letters to find the mystery word.

Word Bank

impulses	feelings	laziness	thoughts	words
internal	greedy	temper	wants	

---

1. If you don't like to work and you'd rather sleep all day, you'll be known for your
(O)__ __ __ __ __ __ __ __.

2. Everyone has fleeting __ __ (O) __ __ __ __ __ and strong
__ __ __ (O) __ __ __ __ that can sometimes get us in trouble.

3. Self-discipline means using an __ __ __ __ (O) __ __ __ set of rules to control your actions (means "inside you").

4. Things we long for that are not *needs* are (O) __ __ __ __.

5. Sometimes we need strong (O) __ __ __ __ to express strong feelings.

6. __ __ (O) __ __ __ people want everything for themselves and nothing for others.

7. When someone makes you mad, don't lose your __ __ __ (O) __ __!

8. Urges that tempt you to make unwise or hurtful choices are called
(O) __ __ __ __ __ __ __.

Unscramble the circled letters to find the mystery word and write it below.
Another word for self-discipline is:

__ __ __ __ __ __ __ __ __

8 Fairness

Fairness means avoiding prejudice, seeking justice and playing by the rules. It means making sure everyone gets a fair share. People who are fair understand that each person is valuable and deserves to have an equal chance for the good things in life. They stand up for every person's right to have his basic needs met, and to defend himself. Learning to share and cooperate with others is a big part of becoming a fair person. The Golden Rule, "Treat others as you wish to be treated," is all about being fair. Fairness and justice are so important to the way people get along that we find stories about them in every country, culture and faith tradition throughout history.

You show *fairness* when you:

- do your share of the chores at home because you helped make the mess.

- refuse to gossip; find out for yourself what's true.

- treat people as individuals, rather than as part of a group.

- share the cookies evenly with your brothers and sisters.

- play games by the rules and make sure the same rules apply to everyone.

- choose a movie based on everyone's opinions; find one that's OK with everyone.

■ *Bernard* by Bernard Waber. Houghton Mifflin Company, 1990. K–3. When Bernard's people decide to split up, they argue over who gets the dog, and expect Bernard to choose between them. Instead, he runs away to find a new home. At the end of a luckless day, his people find him. The story ends unresolved, but the couple agrees the solution must be what's best for Bernard. This thinly disguised divorce/custody story may resonate with some students.

■ *The Cow of No Color* by Nina Jaffe and Steve Zeitlin. Henry Holt and Company, 1998. K–5. Jaffe and Zeitlin give us a wonderful collection of stories from around the world that challenge us to ponder what is just and fair. Some are presented as riddles and invite reflection. They may be used individually, as teasers or Information to Share, or assigned as a package to older readers. You might read and discuss one story each day that you work on this chapter.

■ *The Crack-of-Dawn Walkers* by Amy Hest. Macmillan Publishing Company, 1984. K–3. Every Sunday morning, Grandfather takes an early morning walk. Sadie and brother Ben decide to trade weeks, so each gets private time with him, to reminisce about the Old Country and build new memories. A sweet story about sharing and fairness in a family.

■ *Dare to Dream: Coretta Scott King and the Civil Rights Movement* by Angela Medearis. Lodestar Books, 1994. 4–6. This biography highlights King's life and her work with her husband, Martin Luther King, Jr., from her Alabama childhood until publication. King's courage, determination and self-sacrifice in pursuit of her dream of a more just and peaceful world are evident throughout.

■ *The Doorbell Rang* by Pat Hutchins. William Morrow, 1994. K–3. Nobody makes cookies better than Grandma, but Sam and Victoria are happy to share a fresh batch made by Ma. Six each, until the doorbell rings, and then rings again, and again… Finally, who's at the door to save the day?

■ *Economic Causes* by Kathy Katella-Cofrancesco. Twenty-First Century Books, 1998. 3–5. This title in the Celebrity Activist series describes thirteen charitable organizations and their celebrity supporters. The celebrities, having found success and prosperity, choose to help meet the needs of people who are struggling for the basics in life. Bruce Springsteen expresses the spirit of the book: "Economic injustice falls on everybody's head and steals everyone's freedom." Short chapters make this book versatile for use in the classroom.

■ *How My Parents Learned to Eat* by Ina R. Friedman. Houghton Mifflin Company, 1984. K–3. A Japanese American girl tells how her American father and Japanese mother got together. They each feared that their different customs (i.e. eating with chopsticks vs. flatware) might cause problems. But their willingness to compromise and find fair solutions hints at the future success of their marriage.

■ *The Journal of Ben Uchida, Citizen 13559, Mirror Lake Internment Camp* by Barry Denenberg. Scholastic, 1999. 4–5. This fictional My Name is America series title reads like nonfiction. It personalizes one of the most shameful occurrences in U.S. history, as Ben shares his experiences in the days and months after the bombing of Pearl Harbor. His father is taken away by the FBI, and the rest of his family, with many others, are shipped off to a Japanese internment camp. A powerful depiction of institutionalized prejudice and injustice.

■ *Loudmouth George and the New Neighbors* by Nancy Carlson. Lerner, 1997. 1–2. George doesn't want to know the new neighbors. They're pigs! But when everyone else is having fun, he changes his tune. By the time the cat family moves in, George has learned to give them a chance and treat them as individuals.

■ *Nabulela* by Fiona Moodie. Farrar, Straus and Giroux, 1996. K–3. Nabulela, a sea monster, is terrorizing the people of the nearby village. When the girls of the village are unfair and cruel to Nandi, the favored daughter of the tribal chief, they are charged to defeat Nabulela to pay for their wrongdoing.

■ *No Fair!* by Caren Holtzman. Scholastic: 1997. This Hello Math Reader series title looks at mathematical probability in the context of two young friends, trying to decide what and where to play, and how to share treats fairly. Interesting activities at the end illustrate and apply math concepts.

■ *Shadow Dance* by Tololwa M. Mollel. Clarion Books, 1998. K–5. Salome saves a crocodile trapped in the weeds, only to be captured in turn by the ungrateful animal for lunch. Salome argues for justice, but several "impartial" parties refuse to help her. Finally, she finds a friend who helps her turn the tables and beat the crocodile at his own game.

- *Stay Away from Simon!* by Carol Carrick. Econo-Clad, 1999. 1–3. Lucy, like the other children in their town, is repelled and frightened by Simon, who is slow-witted and strange. Whispered stories depict him as dangerous, even evil. But when Lucy and her brother get lost in a snowstorm, Simon finds them and leads them home. An honest, appealing story about differences, gossip, and fair judgment.

- *Stone Soup* retold by Heather Forest. August House Littlefolk, 1998. K–5. Villagers snub two hungry travelers when they ask for food. But they are intrigued when the strangers request a pot to make everyone a feast of soup made from a magic stone. The result is a tasty lesson in the magic of sharing for the common good. Recipe at the end.

- *This is Our House* by Michael Rosen. Candlewick Press, 1996. K–2. George has a cardboard box house, but he's decided to keep it to himself and not let anyone else in. "Not for girls, twins, people with glasses…" That is, until HE gets left out. Then he finds a new perspective on not only what's fair, but also what's fun!

- *The War with Grandpa* by Robert Kimmel Smith. Econo-Clad, 1999. 3–5. Peter loves his Grandpa, who has been lonely and sad since Grandma died. He's glad he's coming to live with the family—until he learns that Grandpa will take over his room! Peter decides to stand up for himself, and declares a war (of practical jokes and minor harassment) to win back his room. To his surprise, Grandpa gets into the "war" in a way that helps him reconnect with the world, and helps Peter find a solution that's fair to everyone.

- *The Well* by Mildred D. Taylor. Dial Books for Young Readers, 1995. 3–5. This story tells of a drought summer in Mississippi in the early 1900s, when the only sweet well belongs to the Logans, a black family who share freely with all who need, regardless of color. Despite their generosity, the Logans are looked down upon and ill-treated by one

family in particular, because of their color. A painful and dangerous series of encounters barely avoids turning into full-blown tragedy, through what amounts to a glimpse, at least, of justice.

- *Zinnia and Dot* by Lisa Campbell Ernst. Penguin Putnam, 1995. K–3. Zinnia and Dot each thinks she is the most beautiful hen in the coop, and her eggs are the best. They bicker and brag until a weasel sneaks into the coop and steals all the eggs, except one. Faced with the mystery of whose egg it is, they grudgingly agree to share its care until it hatches. The bickering doesn't stop, but when the weasel returns to threaten their precious egg, the two team up in defense. In the end, they settle on a surprising, but just and satisfying, solution.

Other Media

- *Dr. Seuss: Yertle the Turtle* adapted from the Dr. Seuss story, narrated by John Lithgow. Sony, 1991 (videocassette). K–5. The Turtle King of Sala-ma-Sond decides it's not enough to be king of the little pond he views from his rock. He is undisputed ruler of all he can see, so he must see more. How? By climbing up a tower made of his subject turtles! The hardship on the poor turtles below and the undignified end to the King's unjust ambitions are shared with Seuss' characteristic light-hearted morality.

- *Golden Rule* designed by Jeffrey Streiff. Special Ideas, 1991 (poster). K–5. This poster shows five children from different cultures praying in different ways, illustrating expressions of the Golden Rule from Buddhist, Jewish, Christian, Muslim and Baha'i scriptures. A nice way to emphasize the primacy of this concept across times, places and religions. Available through Special Ideas, www.special-ideas.com.

- "Stone Soup" by Marcia Brown, from *The Amazing Bone and other Caldecott Classics*. Weston Woods, 1996 (videocassette). This Caldecott Honor version tells the French tale retold in the book by the same name above. The two could be used together to compare versions, or as indicated in the Activities section below.

Fairness Activities

Discussion Prompts

Use these prompts to explore the concept of fairness.

▲ **Fair Characters.** Read *Nabulela* with the class. Discuss these questions:

  • Who in the story acted with fairness? When?

  • Who in the story acted unfairly? When?

  • How would the story be different if the chief had not favored his daughter so much over the other girls?

  • How would the story be different if the girls hadn't put Nandi in danger out of jealousy?

  • Do you think that acting fairly in the first place can save you from having to accept a just punishment later? Give examples.

▲ **"Their Own Medicine" vs. The Golden Rule.** Compare and contrast these two approaches to fairness. Start by reviewing stories from the first chapter of *The Cow of No Color*, or *Shadow Dance*.

  • What does it mean to "give someone a taste of his own medicine?" How is this fair? Does it help teach the person to be fairer next time? If your students are mature enough to not use names or hurt feelings, invite them to give examples from their own experience.

Next, review with students the poster about The Golden Rule (see "Other Media" under "Fairness Resources on previous page). Or, write the Golden Rule on the board.

  • What is the Golden Rule? Can you say it in your own words?

  • How does the Golden Rule express fairness?

  • How are these two approaches to fairness similar? How are they different?

  • Which one do you think might be more effective in teaching fairness and justice? Does it depend on the situation? Why?

  • Which do you think is harder to do: Respond toward mean people with the same hurtfulness, or treat them the way you'd like to be treated? Again, if you can do so without threatening emotional safety in the classroom, invite examples.

▲ **Prejudice/Stereotypes.** A stereotype is an idea that is used to describe a whole group of people collectively, without considering their individuality. Give examples (Girls are weaker than boys, Asians are smart in math, etc.). Prejudice means making up your mind about people before knowing the facts, because they are part of a particular group. Stereotypes or prejudices may be insulting or flattering, but they're always unfair, because they don't take into account the individual. In *Loudmouth George and the New Neighbors*, George doesn't want to meet the new neighbors, because they are pigs. In *This is Our House*, George doesn't want to let in girls, small people, people with glasses, etc. Pose these questions:

  • Have you ever felt someone disliked you, or wouldn't give you a chance, because you were part of a certain group? (Girls or boys, African American or Latino, too young or too old, special needs, etc.) How did that feel?

  • Have you ever felt uncomfortable with someone you didn't know because he or she looked a certain way, talked a certain way, or was part of a certain group? Did your feelings change once you got to know that person as an individual?

  • We're all part of different groups. We're part of families, schools, nationalities, age groups, etc. But we're individuals, too. Are you just like your brother or sister? Would you want people to think you're just like all other people your age that they know? Or your race? Or hair color? Why is it unfair to judge a person as part of a group, before you know him or her?

Games

Use these games when students need a change of pace or a break from the work of the day.

▲ **Acrostic Puzzle.** This is a word puzzle that can be read up, down and across. The letters of a word or name, written vertically, are used in other words or phrases written horizontally, to create a meaningful composition. Depending on the ages and skill levels in your class, this puzzle can be used in different ways. You might simply write it on the board, read it to the class, and talk about both the acrostic form and what each word has to do with fairness. You might use the handout on p. 69 to review the sample, and then create an acrostic as a class. Or, you might use the handout to assign individual students to create their own compositions to share with the class.

▲ **"Fair to Whom?"** This game gets students thinking about fairness and sharing in very concrete terms. You'll need a bag of individually wrapped candy with enough pieces to give each student four, and enough decks of cards to give each student one card showing a joker, or a number from ace (one) through four. Shuffle your cards well. Tell the class you have a special treat to share today. Have each student pick a card. Start back at the beginning, and give each student candy to correspond with his or her card: None for jokers, and 1–4 pieces for aces through fours. Allow a short time for students to react to the distribution. Use your judgment about when to refocus the group, using these prompts:

• Those who got 4s, stand. How did you feel when you drew your card and got your candy? What did you do next?

• Those who got jokers, stand. How did you feel? What did you do?

• Was this a fair way to distribute the candy? Why or why not? What would have made it fairer?

• What can we do now to make the situation fairer?

If some of your students shared spontaneously, thank them for their sense of fairness. Then go around and equalize the candy to four pieces each, based on each student's card. Remind any who received candy from classmates the first round to return it the second round!

▲ **Cheating.** Play a game you normally have in the classroom, but deliberately create an unfair situation by changing the rules during the game, favoring one team or player, etc. If you made the board game in the chapter on Perseverance, you might arbitrarily let one player roll three dice instead of two each turn, require another player to draw sad face cards every turn, or announce that all blond players must sit out the next turn. Sometime between the onset of frustration and outright mutiny, stop the game and talk about how it's working and why. Help students see how cheating or unfair rules ruin the game for everyone by removing the challenge and the chance for any player to win. Then give them a chance to play the game correctly.

Creative Expressions

Have fun with these creative ways to process concepts from the books on the list.

▲ **Problem Solving.** Give examples from the stories (*The Cow of No Color*, especially the story on p. 118, *The Crack-of-Dawn Walkers*, and *How My Parents Learned to Eat* are good resources) of fair and unfair ways to make everyday decisions. Then divide the class into groups, and give them each a scenario. For example, you might tell one group, "Your parents have $10 per week they can spend on allowances for you and your brother and sister. How should they split up the money?" Or "You hear a rumor that a classmate you thought was your friend said something mean about you. What will you do?" Or "You got caught pinching your little brother. What should your punishment be?" Each group must discuss the situation, and come up with both an unfair and a fair way to solve the problem, and act them out for the class. Have them explain why the second solution is fairer.

▲ **Mock Trial.** Hold a mock trial of one of the characters from the stories. For example, you might try George in *This is Our House* for discrimination, the crocodile in *Shadow Dance* for breach of contract or Peter in *The War With Grandpa* for theft. Assign students roles as plaintiff, defendant and counsel for each side, judge or jury. Have students prepare, then present their cases and rebut the opposition. The jury hears the evidence and decides on a verdict. The judge determines the penalty. Discuss how justice was or was not served!

Note: You'll find information on holding mock trials on the American Bar Association web site, *www.abanet.org.* Click "General Public Resources," then "Public Education," "For Educators," "State" and "Common Products." While the scripts are for older students, you might find them helpful and adaptable.

▲ **Cooperating and Sharing.** Watch the video of "Stone Soup," and discuss the concepts of cooperating and sharing for the common good as you cook your own lunch. There's a recipe in the book. You can send a note home with students in advance, explaining the project and asking each student to bring one ingredient for the soup.

▲ **Book Reports.** Assign older students one of these four books: *The Well, The Journal of Ben Uchida, Stay Away from Simon,* or *The War with Grandpa.* Students will write a book report stressing what the book has to say about fairness. Present reports on the same book together, and discuss each book briefly at the end of the reports. Some titles, like *The Journal of Ben Uchida* or *The Well,* may generate serious discussion on important issues of fairness and justice.

Miscellaneous Activities

Try these activities to help students understand the concepts and practice of fairness.

▲ **Suggestion Box.** Create a suggestion box for students to express what they think is or is not fair about life in their classroom, and what could be done to make it fairer. Require that students submit one suggestion for improvement with every complaint they put in the box!

▲ **Classroom Chores.** Discuss and decide together who will do which classroom chores, and when and how. Develop lists and charts of classroom duties to help assign and monitor chores, and to demonstrate fairness in sharing the workload.

▲ **Community Representative.** Invite a guest to the classroom to talk about how his or her work is based on the concept of fairness or justice. You might invite a juvenile or family court judge, family law attorney, social worker or activist for civil rights in the community. Prepare the class to treat the guest with respect and to ask good questions. An older class might take a field trip to visit juvenile or family court in action.

▲ **Advocating for Justice.** Review the book *Economic Causes.* Invite students to research and report on other causes related to justice or equality, and the people who advocate for them. Other interesting issues to research might include the Equal Rights Amendment, Affirmative Action, or Title IX regarding funding for women's sports in higher education.

▲ **Mathematics and Fairness.** A basic premise of deciding what's fair is giving people an equal chance to succeed. Use the activities at the end of *No Fair!* to explore probability as it relates to fairness. You might also use *The Doorbell Rang* to construct word problems about dividing the cookies equally.

▲ **"You Cut, I Pick."** Take the opportunity to use an interesting variety of methods for sharing and choosing fairly in the everyday affairs of the classroom. For example, when two students need to share something equally, employ the "You cut, I pick" method, in which one student divides the material, and the other gets to pick which segment he or she wants. Or, when everyone wants to talk at once, deal out well-shuffled cards from a deck and start with the aces.

Fairness Acrostic Puzzle

Directions: An acrostic puzzle is a word puzzle that can be read up, down and across. The letters of a word or name, written vertically, are used in other words or phrases written horizontally, to create a meaningful composition. Look at the sample puzzle for the word "justice."

```
    JUSTICE  IS...
   TRUTH
   REASONABLE
   RIGHTS
   FAIR
        CONSTITUTIONAL
   LEGAL
```

Now, using the word "fairness" provided below, write your own acrostic composition.

FAIRNESS IS...

```
A
I
R
N
E
S
S
```

9 Friendship

Friendliness means being interested in people and treating them with warmth and courtesy. Smiling, looking people in the eye and saying hello show that you might like to know them better, and let them know you. Being a friend is more personal and lasting. It's a combination of caring, respect, honesty and fairness. A good friend not only likes you, but can be trusted to keep your secrets, stand up for you, make time for you, care how you feel and try to help when you have a problem. Friends invest time and energy in each other, and have interests and activities they share. When they get upset with each other, they work it out. Real friends are happy for each other's success, and help each other be and do their best.

You show *friendship* when you:

- invite a new student to play with you and your friends.

- ask your friend what's wrong when she looks sad.

- call your friend to ask about his vacation, and listen before you talk about yourself.

- make a special present for your friend that's just right for her.

- listen without judging when your friend has done something wrong, and try to help him make it right.

- respect your friend's rights by not borrowing things without permission.

Friendship Resources

■ *And to Think That We Thought We'd Never be Friends* by Mary Ann Hoberman. Crown Publishers, Inc., 1999. K–2. From a sibling battle to a worldwide parade, this riotous celebration of all-embracing friendliness shows how sharing and inviting others in can overcome obstacles and differences, and make friends of strangers. The unifying power of music is featured.

■ *Best Friends* by Loretta Krupinski. Hyperion Books for Children, 1998. K–3. A moving story about how the friendship between pioneer girl, Charlotte, and Nez Perce girl, Lily, in the 1870s helped to free Lily's band of Nez Perce from forced evacuation from their land to a reservation.

■ *The Best Friends Book* by Arlene Erlbach. Free Spirit Publishing Inc., 1995. 3–5. Erlbach features 11 sets of best friends of different ages, with a variety of shared interests and differences. She follows up with suggested activities for friends to enjoy together and advice about making and keeping friends.

■ *Charlotte's Web* by E. B. White. Harper Collins, 1999. K–5. A beloved, classic story of friendship and caring. Fern's love for a runty pig that she rescues is at the center of the Newbery Award Book, which dramatizes love, joy and sacrifice among friends.

■ *Chicken Sunday* by Patricia Polacco. Philomel Books, 1992. K–3. Three children dream of buying their Gramma the Easter bonnet she admires. But they must win over a shopkeeper, who thinks they vandalized his store, to do so. In the process, the children learn about the Old Country, make a new friend, and discover the joy of extending yourself for someone you love.

■ *Dr. Ruth Talks About Grandparents: Advice for Kids on Making the Most of a Special Relationship* by Dr. Ruth K. Westheimer with Pierre A. Lehu. Farrar Straus Giroux, 1997. 3–5. Dr. Ruth makes the case for developing close friendships with grandparents, in a lively, engaging style. She shares interesting, creative suggestions for strengthening ties with grandparents nearby and far away, and also talks about finding "foster grandparents" and dealing with the death of a grandparent.

■ *Fishing for Methuselah* by Roger Roth. HarperCollins, 1998. K–5. Ivan and Olaf are best friends, though you'd never know it from the way they argue and compete. The biggest contest of all is to catch the legendary monster fish, Methuselah. But the competition gets out of hand, and Methuselah himself comes through to save them both. A clever story of friendship, competition and cooperation.

■ *George and Martha Encore* by James Marshall. Econo-Clad, 1999. K–1. Five short, pointed stories about friendship starring the well-known hippo friends. Accessible and appealing for younger students.

■ *The Hating Book* by Charlotte Zolotow. Econo-Clad, 1999. K–2. This sensitive, simple story illustrates how easily rumors can break down a friendship, and how a little fairness and honesty can repair it.

■ *Maebelle's Suitcase* by Tricia Tusa. Econo-Clad, 1999. K–3. Eccentric Maebelle, who lives in a treehouse, thinks fast and creatively to help her bird friend Binkle. It's time to fly south, but he can't seem to leave behind his belongings. This Reading Rainbow title celebrates their quirky, joyful, selfless friendship.

■ *Margaret and Margarita* by Lynn Reiser. Greenwillow Books, 1993. K–2. Margaret and Margarita meet at the park with their mothers. They don't speak each other's languages, but they make friends just the same, sharing their toys and simple words. The encounter leaves both the girls and their mothers eager for their next trip to the park. Nice bilingual (Spanish, English) format.

■ *Mrs. Rose's Garden* by Elaine Greenstein. Simon & Schuster, 1996. K–3. Mrs. Rose yearns to win a blue ribbon at the fair for her vegetables. But the year it looks like she's found the secret and will win them all, she realizes it would be more fun to share the wealth, and secretly transplants from her garden to those of her friends. The success of her plan brings pleasure to Mrs. Rose and her fellow blue-ribbon winners.

■ *One of Each* by Mary Ann Hoberman. Little, Brown and Co., 1997. K–2. Oliver Tolliver loves his neat, orderly home, just for one. In fact, it's so perfect that he wants to show it off. But his guest doesn't feel comfortable in a house just for one. Oliver decides to make room in his life for more than one, and discovers the joys of friendship.

■ *The Pinballs* by Betsy Byars. Harper Collins, 1998. 3–5. Carlie, Harvey and Thomas J. arrive as foster children in the Mason home from different backgrounds of pain, disappointment and loss. All three are damaged, and have their own ways of coping and avoiding pain. But the Masons' gentle caring and Carlie's defiant strength create the beginnings of healing, friendship and a sense of belonging.

- *Thank You, Jackie Robinson* by Barbara Cohen. William Morrow, 1997. 3–5. Sam feels alone in the depth of his devotion to the Dodgers, until he meets the new cook at his Mom's Inn. Davey is a large, sixty-year-old black man—not the obvious candidate for best friend to scrawny, shy, white, 10-year-old Sam, who keeps to himself and fears strangers. But the two form a deep bond. When Sam needs to offer a gift of love to his dying friend, he finds the ability to stretch himself in ways he never thought possible. Full of baseball action and powerful messages about prejudice, love, friendship and grief.

- *The View from Saturday* by E. L. Konigsburg. Aladdin Paperbacks, 1996. 3–5. Four very different sixth graders come together, through a combination of chance and circumstances, to forge profound friendships and win an academic competition. They are able to reach beyond conventional limits between cultures and generations with humor, intelligence and generosity. A Newbery Award Book.

Other Media

- *The Cricket in Times Square* by George Selden. Bantam Doubleday Dell Audio, 1995 (audiobook). 2–5. The Newbery Honor Book is beautifully performed by Rene Auberjonois. Chester the Cricket is transported to Times Square subway station by accident, from his country home in Connecticut. What awaits him there includes adventure, fame for his musical talents, and rich new friendships.

- *Friends Forever.* Walt Disney Records, 1998 (CD). K–3. From jigs to Celtic pipes, from silly to sentimental, these musical odes to friendship should appeal to a range of tastes and serve well as background for projects in the Activities section below.

- *Harriet the Spy* based on the novel by Louise Fitzhugh, adaptation by Greg Taylor and Julie Talen. Paramount Pictures, 1996 (videocassette). 2–5. Harriet prepares to be a writer by spying on people and recording her observations and blunt opinions in a notebook. The notebook is found and read by her classmates, creating chaos, hurt feelings, and complex plans for revenge. The novel was a 1999 Parents Choice title.

Friendship Activities

Discussion Prompts

Use these prompts to explore the concept of friendship.

▲ **"What's Important In a Friend?"** Review your favorite stories from the bibliography that suggest important qualities in friends. *George and Martha Encore, Mrs. Rose's Garden, Charlotte's Web,* or *Maebelle's Suitcase* are good choices. Discuss what students look for in a good friend, using these steps:

1) What are the most important qualities for a good friend to have? Brainstorm, listing all ideas on the board. Add your own to make a good list.

2) Have students look at the list of qualities, choose the five that are most important to them, and write them down.

3) Next, circle the five qualities that come up most often on student lists.

4) Ask the students why they feel these qualities are so important in a friend.

5) Remind the class that working to develop these qualities in themselves will make them better friends to others.

▲ **Friends Alike and Different.** Most of your friends may be much like you—similar age, same sex, similar interests and activities. They may even live near you and be in your class at school. But some of the most rewarding friendships can be with people who are different from you. Share examples from *The Best Friends Book*, or review *Chicken Sunday, Margaret and Margarita* or *Thank You, Jackie Robinson* as you discuss, using the following questions:

• How might a friend be different from you? (List answers on the board. They might include different gender, older or younger, physical or learning disabilities, different appearance, different national or cultural background, different religions, etc. They might even mention animal friends.)

• What are the advantages of a friend who is much like you? What are the disadvantages?

• What are the advantages of a friend quite different from you? What are the disadvantages?

• It's easier to find friends similar to yourself. What are some ways you could look for a new friend who's different from you?

▲ **Good Secrets, Bad Secrets.** One thing we all look for in a friend is the ability to share and keep secrets and confidences. It's an important part of the trust in friendships. In *Best Friends*, the secret hiding place Charlotte and Lily share in the doll's head is critical in saving Lily's people. The secret Ivan and Olaf share about their experience in *Fishing for Methuselah* strengthens their friendship and allows them to work together, for a change. And Mr. and Mrs. Rose's secret in *Mrs. Rose's Garden* brings them and others great pleasure. But secrets can be harmful, too. In *The Hating Book*, whispered rumors divide best friends. And Harriet's private opinions, written down and then discovered by her classmates in *Harriet the Spy*, cause all kinds of problems and hurt feelings. Talk with the class about secrets, using these prompts:

• What kinds of secrets do you like to share with your close friends?

• Without revealing the secrets, share examples of the kinds of secrets that strengthen friendships without harming anyone. (Children might mention a special place they like to go, a secret code they use, gifts or surprises for their friends or confidences about people and activities they share.)

• What kinds of secrets might be dangerous or harmful? (Include gossip that hurts people's feelings, secrets about violence or inappropriate touch or confided feelings of depression and worthlessness.)

Point out that good friends have a responsibility to help keep their friends from hurting themselves or others, or from being hurt by others, and that it is at least as important as their responsibility to keep a secret. A good guideline is this: if someone is being hurt or might be hurt, it's a dangerous secret and should be told to a trusted adult.

Games

Use these games when students need a change of pace or a break from the work of the day.

▲ **Word Scramble.** p. 76.

▲ **"To Know Me Is to Love Me!"** The first step toward making a friend is getting to know someone better, and most people have at least one appealing quality or interest that could form the starting point for a friendship. In *The Pinballs*, the three children seem to have little in common, but become friends as they learn more about each others' experiences. Try this game to help students learn new things about each other. You'll need small balloons—one for each student—and small slips of paper. *Hint: to help assure anonymity, you may want to use balloons that are all one color.*

• Give each student a balloon and a slip of paper. Have them write on the paper one good thing about themselves (a quality, talent, interest or experience) that most people don't know about. No names on the papers! Then have them fold or roll the paper, slip it into the balloon, and blow up and tie the balloon.

• Throw the balloons in a corner of the room.

• One by one, have students choose a balloon, pop it, and read out loud the information on the paper. Students have three chances to guess which student wrote the slip. If they don't guess, the student must identify himself or herself.

• If there is time, you might have some students tell a bit more about particularly interesting information on the slips, but be careful not to leave some students feeling favored and others left out.

Creative Expressions

Have fun with these creative ways to process concepts from the books on the list.

▲ **Friendship Bracelets.** Using the directions on pages 61–62 of *The Best Friends Book*, have each student make a bracelet. Use an average length for the thread, so any bracelet will fit any student. Then, using pairs of matching cards from two decks of playing cards, well shuffled, deal out the cards and have each student find the student with the matching card. These students will tie their bracelets on each other's wrists.

▲ **"Celebrating Friendship" Slide Show.** Create a slide show to show another class, or perhaps the whole school at an assembly. Have each student contribute at least one slide. Use a combination of slide photographs of friends doing things together, other illustrations, written captions and slogans or quotations about friendship. To create the non-photographic slides, use this process:

1) Gather old slides that you no longer need.

2) Soak the photographic surface in warm water for 1–2 minutes, and then scrape off the image with a sharp knife. Plastic-mounted slides can be immersed in water as they are. Cardboard-mounted slides must be removed from the mounts, "erased" with water and

scraping and taped back into their mounts.

3) Use the "erased" slides as blanks, for students to add words or pictures using fine-tipped felt markers or poster paint and small brushes. This is fine work on a small surface, so keep expectations realistic.

4) Once you've put together your slide show, add popular songs about friendship as background (You might use tracks from the *Friends Forever* CD), and dim the lights!

▲ **Acrostic Poems.** In acrostic poems or puzzles, the letters of a word or name, written vertically, are used in other words or phrases written horizontally, to create a meaningful composition. Invite students to create acrostic poems about their friends, using their names as in the example below using the name, "Connor." The poems might make good gifts. Remind them to consider family members, too.

Caring
Outgoing
Never cruel
Nice to everyone
Optimistic
Responsible

▲ **Book Talks.** Assign older students to read *Charlotte's Web*; *The Pinballs*; *Thank You, Jackie Robinson*; or *The View from Saturday*. Students will prepare a brief (1–2 minute) talk for the class, designed to entice others to read the book. Book talks are similar to oral book reports, but may be less complete and analytical, and more entertaining, ending with a cliffhanger that will make students want to read more! A fun follow-up activity might be to poll the class to see who plans to read which book, based on which book talk.

Miscellaneous Activities

Try these activities to help students understand the concepts and practice of friendship.

▲ **Pen Pals.** Connect kids with pen pals from other parts of the world using one of these services:

Peace Pals
26 Benton Rd.
Wassaic, NY 12592
845-877-6093
www.theworldpeacesanctuary.org

World Pen Pals
P.O. Box 337
Saugerties, NY 12477
845-246-7828
www.world-pen-pals.com

▲ **The Science of Friendship: Experiments with Magnets.** Try these experiments. You might either present the friendship principle before each experiment, or do the experiment and ask students to guess what ideas the experiment might demonstrate about friendship.

• Principle: "Most people can be friendly with one another, but it takes a special attraction to make close friends. Without that 'chemistry,' you can't force a friendship to happen." You'll need two disk magnets and a vertical stand on a base. Slip the magnets over the stand with their north poles facing each other. (See illustration below.) What happens? Can you push them together? How much force does it take? Do they stay together when you let go? Can you force the top magnet over the top of the stand by moving the bottom magnet?

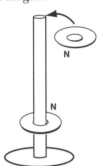

• Principle: "People with the right things in common to be good friends will find each other, even in a crowd." You'll need a bar magnet, a plastic sandwich bag, a teaspoon of salt, and a pinch of iron filings. Shake the salt and iron filings together in the sealed bag. Rub the magnet on the outside of the bag. What happens? Can you separate the iron completely from the salt?

• Principle: "Good friends can pick each other up when they're feeling down, and help each other rise above their lower impulses and 'do the right thing.'" You'll need two bar magnets and a safety pin. Lay one magnet on a table. Set the safety pin perpendicularly across the magnet. While holding the bottom magnet, move the second magnet toward the pin until it touches the top, and raise it above the first magnet. What happens? Can you lift the pin completely off the bottom magnet?

• Principle: "Too much fighting and conflict can destroy friendships." You'll need a bar magnet, an iron nail, a safety pin, some tape and a hammer. Lay the nail on top of the magnet for a few minutes, to magnetize it. Show how the magnetized nail attracts and holds the safety pin. Then secure the nail on a wooden surface with tape, with the point of the nail facing east, and hit it 25–30 times with the hammer. Try again to use the nail as a magnet to attract and hold the safety pin. What happens?

You might want to discuss both the science of magnets and friendship in greater depth as you do these experiments. You could talk about how the friendship principle is demonstrated, and what aspects of friendship are represented by items used in the experiment.

▲ **Friendship Across Generations.** Review *Dr. Ruth Talks about Grandparents.* Assign students to interview an elderly person, preferably a grandparent, about friendship. Work together to develop questions to guide the interviews. Here are some examples:

• Who were your best friends when you were growing up?

• What kinds of things did you do together?

• What was important to you in a friend?

• Who are your best friends now?

• What do you do together?

• What are the most important things to look for in a friend?

Interviews can be in person, or via telephone or e-mail. Encourage in-person or phone interviews, for more personal interaction. Students who don't have grandparents available might choose an elderly neighbor or friend, or ask their parents to help them identify someone at a senior citizen center or housing facility who would enjoy a visit. Have students take notes or record their interviews on audio or videotape, and create a written report or edited media presentation for the class. Discuss students' experiences with this project. Did the project help them strengthen a friendship or make a new friend?

Note: Parents might have to help younger students complete the interview and presentation.

▲ **Friendship Survey.** Survey the class about friendship, using the questionnaire on page 77. With younger students, you might send the questionnaire home and ask parents to help complete them. For a larger sample, you might assign each student to complete a form and also survey two other people in the school or at home. Compile and discuss the results. Consider reporting the results in a school newspaper or special report. Everyone is interested in friendship!

Friendship Word Scramble

Directions: Unscramble the following words related to friendship by drawing lines between the scrambled word and its unscrambled match.

icngar	trust
netyhso	caring
screept	respect
irsghna	unselfish
cripyva	cooperation
srtut	compromise
cratonpioeo	differences
emsciropmo	sharing
elhnusifs	honesty
dreefcenfis	privacy

Friendship Survey

Directions: Please fill out this survey as completely as possible. You don't need to put your name on it. ***Thank You!***

- Your age and grade at school: _____

- Are you male _____ or female _____?

- Are you a person who has many casual friends _____? Or are you a person with a few very close friends _____?

- Do you have a best friend? _____

- Is your closest friend the same sex as you? _____

- Is your closest friend within a year of your age _____? Within two years _____? Within five years _____? Much older or younger than you_____?

- Do you have any close friends 10 years or more older or younger than you? _____

- What do you think is the most important quality in a good friend? _____
_____

- What's your favorite thing to do with your friends? _____
_____

- How are your closest friends similar to you? _____
_____

- How are your closest friends different from you? _____
_____

- Have you made a new close friend in the last year? _____

- Where have you found most of your close friends (at school, in the neighborhood, in a religious community, etc.)? _____

- Are any of your close friends family members or relatives? _____ If so, how are these friends related to you (sister, cousin, grandparent, etc.)? _____

- Would you like to have more friends? _____

10 Citizenship

A *citizen* is a full member of a community or nation, entitled to all the benefits and protection of that community. "Citizenship" is about how we respond to that membership. Whether we're talking about our families, neighborhoods, school communities, states, nation or world, we need to think about our attitudes and actions. Do we notice and appreciate the benefits of citizenship? Do we get involved in our communities, caring and contributing for the good of all? Do we feel responsible for speaking out against injustice and making our communities better? Every quality already discussed in this book is important as we try to be good citizens of our local, national and global communities.

You are being a good *citizen* when you:

- stand respectfully for the singing of the national anthem.

- speak out against unfair policies at school or in the community.

- volunteer at a local animal shelter or visit senior citizens in a nursing home.

- encourage classmates who are struggling to work out their differences and get along.

- write a letter of thanks to your parents, teacher or someone in the community who helps you learn, grow and stay safe.

- "reduce, reuse and recycle" to help protect the environment.

- ask your parents' opinions on election issues and encourage them to vote.

- obey the law and the rules—even when no one is watching!

Citizenship Resources

- *The American Wei* by Marion Hess Pomeranc. Albert Whitman & Co., 1998. K–3. It's naturalization day for Wei Fong and his family, along with many others. This book shares the process of naturalization, through the eyes of one child and family. This is a nice look at the diversity of backgrounds among American citizens, and the hope and idealism with which immigrants embrace their new country.

- *Blodwen and the Guardians* by David Wiseman. Houghton Mifflin Company, 1983. 3–5. Blodwen and her family move to a cottage in the country, bordered by a mysterious grove that both attracts and frightens her. The grove hides a burial mound for an ancient king, and is protected by the mythical Guardians, who are the subject of half-remembered legends and superstition about the "little folk." When road construction threatens both the peace and beauty of the village, and the sacred grove, the Guardians must make allies of the dreaded humans. An enchanting story of mystery, sacredness, "progress" versus the environment, and the power of collective action.

- *Celebrating America: A Collection of Poems and Images of the American Spirit* compiled by Laura Whipple. Philomel Books, 1994. K–5. This collection of poetry and images from the Art Institute of Chicago celebrates the American spirit. Particularly the chapters entitled "Stories" and "Heart" could be well used, in bits and pieces, to help students tune into the history and the diversity of viewpoints and dreams that inspire loyalty in American citizens.

- *Dinah for President* by Claudia Mills. Macmillan Publishing Company, 1992. 3–5. "Dynamite Dinah" loves the spotlight. Upon entering middle school, Dinah decides it's only right that she run for sixth grade president. But when Dinah is forced to define a platform for her campaign, and to help her mother assist an elderly woman to stay in her home, she discovers that her new-found cause (recycling) and new-found friend are more important to her than being president.

- *Disappearing Ducks* by Phyllis Reynolds Naylor. Atheneum Books for Young Readers, 1997. K–2. Willie takes responsibility and speaks up when he discovers that ducklings in the motel yard are falling into a storm drain. While the grownups don't want to be bothered, Willie insists that the ducks "belong to all of us," and enlists their help in a rescue mission.

- *Granddaddy's Gift* by Margaree King Mitchell. BridgeWater Books, 1997. K–5. Little Joe learns important lessons from her Granddaddy, the first African-American man to become a registered voter in their Mississippi town. A story of courageous determination to make one's voice heard and to make things better for oneself and others.

- *I Got Community* by Melrose Cooper. Henry Holt and Company, 1995. K–3. Bright, joyful illustrations, rhymes and slangy street rhythms pulse through this book, which celebrates the people that are important in a child's world. The clear message: I count on you, and you can count on me!

- *It Takes a Village* by Jane Cowen-Fletcher. Scholastic, Inc., 1994. K–3. It's market day, and Yemi is proud to be trusted to take care of her little brother "all by herself." When Kokou wanders off, Yemi learns how many people are really there to help each other, how much we count on each other, and how easy it is to take for granted the blessings of shared effort and responsibility in our communities.

- *The Kid's Guide to Service Projects* by Barbara A. Lewis. Free Spirit Publications, 1995. 2–5. This upbeat guide empowers kids to get involved in their communities through volunteering and service projects. Good, practical advice addresses topics ranging from environmental projects to senior citizens, from literacy to feeding the hungry.

- *The Kid's Guide to Social Action* by Barbara A. Lewis. Free Spirit Publications, 1991. 2–5. With the same upbeat, energetic tone as the Kid's Guide… above, Lewis empowers kids to "be heard" in their communities today, and participate in the process of shaping the world they'll live in tomorrow. It's full of encouraging stories of kids' accomplishments and practical advice on how to identify a problem, how to research, brainstorm solutions, plan for practical action, and make your voice heard in effective ways. Lewis insists that no project is too small or too big for kids to tackle. Lots of resources, reproducible worksheets and other tools.

- *Laws* by Zachary A. Kelly. Rourke Corporation, Inc., 1997. K–5. This Law and Order series title looks at why we have laws and how they are made and enforced. It addresses state and local laws, as well as federal, and talks about the rights of both victims and the accused.

- *Sidewalk Trip* by Patricia Hubbell. Harper Festival, 1999. K–2. This very simple rhyming story of a walk in the city shows many of the amenities and services we take for granted in our communities. Shared with younger students, it could help children identify and appreciate the benefits of living together cooperatively.

- *Swimmy* by Leo Lionni. Econo-Clad, 1999. K–3. Swimmy learns the hard way that small fish can be victims in the big sea, losing all his playmates to a big, hungry tuna. His new playmates are afraid to leave their sheltered pool for fear of a similar fate. Swimmy saves the day and improves life for all the little fish when he shows them how to band together for mutual protection. A nice look at the benefits of cooperation and community.

- *The United Nations* by Ann Armbruster. Franklin Watts: 1995. 2–5. Nicely illustrated with photographs, this title traces the world's "only international organization dedicated to peace, justice, and economic equality" from its inception to the near present. It honestly presents the UN's great successes, struggles and failures and the uneven support of its members, as well as its potential for effectiveness in a rapidly changing world.

- *The Voice of the People: American Democracy in Action* by Betsy Maestro. Lothrop, Lee & Shepard Books, 1996. 2–5. A combination of comprehensive overview and fascinating detail, this title summarizes how the United States government is structured and organized, how it operates and changes, and how it reflects the will of the people. An excellent and engaging civics primer.

- *What's an Average Kid Like Me Doing Way up Here?* by Ivy Ruckman. Delacorte Press, 1983. 3–5. "Normal Norman" has plenty on his mind already—his Dad "on leave" from the family to climb mountains, and his first serious crush—when he learns his middle school will be closed to save money. A combination of worry, outrage and a need to impress Lisa trigger the latent activist in Norman, who conspires with a teacher to save the school.

- *When the Monkeys Came Back* by Kristine L. Franklin. Atheneum, 1994. K–5. Set in Costa Rica, this picture book tells of Marta, whose deep respect and love for the life of the forest and the monkeys it houses cause her to break with tradition and devote her life to restoring the rich forest life of her childhood days.

- *Woodrow Wilson* by Alice Osinski. Children's Press, Inc., 1989. 3–5. This Encyclopedia of Presidents title explores the life and leadership of President Wilson, whose "Fourteen Points" for peace after World War I resulted in the establishment of the League of Nations, precursor to the United Nations. While picturing Wilson's weaknesses as a student and problems with ill health, the author shows how Wilson's natural leadership abilities and passion for peace for all the world's people made him a Nobel Peace prizewinner and an exemplary world citizen.

Other Media

- *Millennium Celebration.* Walt Disney Records, 1999 (CD). K–5. This stirring music was written for the spectacular Millennium parade performed twice daily in the Disney theme parks during 1999 and 2000. A combination of vocal and instrumental pieces, it inspires a unifying sense of accomplishment, hope and shared destiny for us as world's citizens.

- *Patriotic Songs & Marches* musical arrangements by Dennis Buck. Kimbo Educational, 1991 (audiocassette). K–5. These enthusiastic renditions of old patriotic standards make your feet itch to march and invite a flag-waving parade. A combination of solos, chorus work and instrumental marches, the tape could be used as background or for sing-along breaks.

Citizenship Activities

Discussion Prompts

Use these prompts to explore the concept of citizenship.

▲ **You are a Citizen of What Communities?** Brainstorm with the class what groups and communities they belong to as citizens (refer to the definition at the beginning of the chapter).

• List ideas on the board. They might include families, classrooms and schools, neighborhoods, religious communities, town, state, country and the world.

• What do these different communities have in common (people working together for the common good, sharing resources, helping each other, trusting each other, etc.)?

• How do we participate in each of these communities?

• You might follow up this discussion with the "My Communities" worksheet on pp. 84–85.

▲ **The Benefits of Citizenship.** Page through the book *Sidewalk Trip*, using the pictures to help students think of services and protection we have living together in communities that we wouldn't have if we lived all alone. (For example, fire hydrants mean fire protection, the ice cream truck, crossing guards, the park.) List ideas on the board. Then go beyond the book to list other benefits and services provided by our communities. If you need further prompts, you might put some items in a bag for students to draw out and guess what service is intended. (For example, toy handcuffs to indicate police protection, a stamp for postal service, a garbage bag for garbage pick-up.) Point out that many of these services are provided by government and paid for by taxes; others are provided as private businesses, possible only when many people live close together in communities.

▲ **Rules and Laws.** Review the book *Laws* with students. Discuss using these questions:

• What is a rule? What do we mean by a law?

• Why do we need rules and laws?

• What are some rules we must follow in the classroom? At home?

• What are some laws we must obey in our town, state, or nation?

• What happens when we don't follow the rules and obey the laws?

▲ **Qualities of a Good Citizen.** Divide the class into nine small groups. Assign each group one of the qualities explored in previous chapters of this book. Each group will discuss what their assigned quality has to do with citizenship, and come up with a paragraph explaining how that quality contributes to good citizenship. Encourage students to cite examples from the stories that support their conclusions. Each group will present their statement to the class.

Games

Use these games when students need a change of pace or a break from the work of the day.

▲ **Word Search.** p. 86.

▲ **Safety in Numbers.** A quick, simple game. Read *Swimmy* with the class, and talk about how Swimmy's clever plan allowed the fish to travel in safety. Then number off the class into "ones" and "twos," and regroup into two teams. Set a timer, giving teams 5 minutes to list as many ideas as they can of ways that living together in communities makes us safer than we would be alone. (Examples: Communities provide police and fire protection, ambulance service, and medical care; we have the military to protect us; streetlights make it safer to walk at night.) Have each group read their list, and compare the two. Members of the team that came up with more good examples might be excused for recess first, or go to the head of the class line for lunch.

▲ **Voting with Marbles.** This game will get students thinking, moving and learning that their votes count! Start by reviewing *Granddaddy's Gift*, and talking about the important privilege and responsibility of participating in your communities with your vote. You'll need paper, crayons or markers, 10 medium-sized containers and enough marbles for each student to have five.

1) Brainstorm ideas about problems that need attention in your school, neighborhood or town. You might use the list on page 16 of *The Kid's Guide to Social Action* to identify possible areas of concern. Problems may be as small as complaints about lunchroom menus, or as big as concern about gang activity or the treat-

ment of minorities by police. Keep going until you have identified 10 varied, specific, locally relevant problems.

2) Write (or draw, depending on grade level) each problem clearly on a sheet of paper, and distribute the papers, with attached containers, around the room.

3) Give each student five marbles.

4) Have students move around the room, considering each problem carefully, and voting for those they feel are most important by placing marbles in their containers. Students may vote for five different problems they think are important, or they may put more than one marble in a given container. Encourage them to choose carefully, because they will be asked to act on their choices later.

5) When all students have voted, count the marbles in each jar, and identify the 3–5 problems the class considers most important.

6) To continue, see "What Can We Do?" in the Creative Expressions section that follows.

Note: Students interested in the concept of voting might enjoy this web site, which also has a "Teachers Only" section with lots of resources: **Kids Voting USA**, *at www.kidsvotingusa.org.*

Creative Expressions

Have fun with these creative ways to process concepts from the books on the list.

▲ **Citizenship Collage.** Tape up a long roll of brown or butcher paper across a whole wall in the classroom or hallway, at an easy working level for students. Have students bring from home pictures or words cut out from magazines, and clippings from newspapers, that relate to citizenship. They might bring pictures of police officers or elected officials, the state or American flag, etc. Or they might bring articles about city council or school board meetings, laws being considered by the legislature, or reports of social problems and the people trying to solve them. Glue the pictures and clippings on the paper, and fill in with drawings, quotations about citizenship, original slogans, hopes and wishes, etc. Contributions to the collage should be reviewed and approved, and students must work cooperatively to create this picture of

their understanding of the meaning of citizenship. This might be a good ongoing project as you study this chapter.

▲ **"My Communities" Worksheet.** Copy the worksheet on pp. 84–85, and have students complete it using resources in the classroom or the media center, and their own creativity. When everyone is finished, review the information, and let children share their world flag designs and pledge of allegiance compositions.

▲ **"What Can We Do?"** Talk about characters in the books that took action to stop injustice or make things better. Good examples are found in *Swimmy; Disappearing Ducks; When the Monkeys Came Back; Woodrow Wilson; Dinah for President; What's An Average Kid Like Me Doing Way Up Here?* and *Blodwen and the Guardians.* Using the 3–5 problems identified in the Games section above, get students involved in taking action. Divide the class into groups, assigning one problem to each group. The groups will discuss their problem and choose one of the actions below or other creative courses of action, or you might assign an appropriate action for the problem:

• Write a letter to the editor of the local newspaper, or a letter to your legislators, explaining the importance of the problem, suggesting solutions and asking for support. The letter must be respectful and well-written, with attention to good spelling and grammar, clear content and proper letter format.

• Write and record a radio (audiocassette) or television (videocassette) public service announcement of 30 seconds to 2 minutes, calling attention to the problem and promoting a solution or course of action that listeners or viewers can support.

• Plan a community event to increase awareness of the issue and raise funds or support toward a solution.

Make sure that the courses of action proposed by student groups include ways for them to stay involved throughout the process. If possible, let students send their letter, submit their PSA, or host their event!

Note: Students who get excited about student activism might check out this web site, which contains lots of "kid power" success stories and resources for choosing causes and taking action: **Activism 2000**, *at www.youthactivism.com.*

Miscellaneous Activities

Try these activities to help students understand the concepts and practice of citizenship.

▲ **Invited Guest.** Read *The American Wei* with students, and then invite a naturalized citizen to visit the classroom. (Are any of your students the children of naturalized citizens?) Ask your guest to talk about the process of becoming a citizen, and his or her reasons for seeking U.S. citizenship. Encourage students to ask respectful, courteous questions about the immigrant's feelings for both his native land and his adopted country.

▲ **Rights and Responsibilities For Citizens.** Give each student two 4" x 6" index cards. Using books from the bibliography (*The Voice of the People* is a good source), other classroom resources and their own knowledge, assign each student to write on one card a right or privilege we have as citizens of our various communities or nation. On the second card, students must write a responsibility related to the right identified on the first card. You might coach a bit, to be sure some basic rights like those in the Bill of Rights are covered, and that the responsibilities relate to the rights. You might set up an example in chart form, using cards taped or held by mag-nets on an appropriate surface. Head the first column "Rights," and put up a card reading, "We have the right to choose our lawmakers." Head the second column, "Responsibilities," and add this card: "We must learn about the candidates and vote in elections." When students have completed their cards, collect them and shuffle them into "decks" of "Rights" cards and "Responsibilities" cards. One by one, call on students to draw a "Rights" card at random, read it to the class, and search through the "Responsibilities" cards to find a match. Once the match is found, read and understood by the class, the student will add the cards to the appropriate columns on the chart, in matching order. Remember to find a fair method of choosing student order for this activity, as it will become easier over time. The last student will have only one of each kind of card left!

▲ **Field Trip.** Arrange for the class to visit a city council meeting, school board meeting or, if you live near your state capitol, your state legislature in session. Prepare the class to behave respectfully during the meeting or session, and discuss the experience afterwards. What issues were considered? Do students have ideas about how to deal with those issues? Follow up with a thank-you letter from the class, including ideas about the issues discussed, if appropriate.

"My Communities" Worksheet

I'm a member of many communities. As a citizen of those communities, I have rights and responsibilities. One responsibility is to know and to care about my communities. This worksheet will let me share what I've learned about some of my communities.

My Family

- These people are members of my family: _____
  _____

- My family lives all together in one house. Yes _____ No _____

- I spend time living in two or more different homes during the year. Yes __ No __

- One thing I like best about my family: _____

My School

- I go to this school: _____

- My school has students in these grades: _____

- My school colors are: _____

- My school's motto is: _____

- My school's mascot is: _____

My Town or City

- I live in this town or city: _____

- My town has this many people living in it: _____

- My town's mayor is named: _____

- My town's motto or welcome slogan is: _____

My State

- I live in this state: _____

- My state's governor is named: _____

- My state's motto is: _____

- My state's flag looks like this:

My Country

- I live in this country: _____

- The President of my country is named: _____

- I show respect to my country's flag by reciting this: _____
_____

- Our national anthem is called: _____

- My county's flag looks like this:

My World

- I live on this planet: _____

- This is my idea of a good pledge of allegiance for the world: _____
_____
_____
_____

- Here's my design for a flag for us to honor as world citizens:

Citizenship Word Search

Directions: Find and circle the words listed in the word bank below. They may read down or across.

```
Y  T  I  L  I  N  I  S  N  O  P  S  E  R  A
J  N  O  I  T  C  E  T  O  R  P  C  L  I  F
C  O  O  P  E  R  A  T  I  O  N  F  E  G  X
I  C  V  V  O  L  U  N  T  E  E  R  C  H  A
P  N  I  E  S  Y  D  B  U  Q  T  E  T  T  A
T  S  E  T  O  R  P  X  T  U  O  E  I  S  C
C  L  O  E  I  F  W  P  I  A  V  D  O  A  E
E  W  Y  L  T  Z  A  X  T  L  N  O  N  O  O
P  F  A  I  R  N  E  S  S  I  R  M  S  V  Y
S  W  A  L  X  C  D  N  N  T  T  B  C  V  X
E  M  U  M  I  M  F  N  O  Y  Q  X  S  P  S
R  Y  U  T  J  E  L  A  C  Y  G  A  Q  A  J
I  N  S  L  T  X  E  P  V  A  J  I  N  B  M
X  U  Z  X  L  L  F  J  Y  U  A  P  A  O  D
J  S  J  Z  F  R  I  W  G  S  U  U  W  N  Q
```

Word Bank					
citizen	elections	freedom	protection	responsibility	vote
constitution	equality	justice	protest	rights	
cooperation	fairness	laws	respect	volunteer	

Title Index